P9-CDL-659

ECONOMIC CONTROL AND FREE ENTERPRISE

HD 82
F66

ECONOMIC CONTROL AND FREE ENTERPRISE

by

SANFORD FOX

85308

PHILOSOPHICAL LIBRARY
New York

Copyright, 1963, by

Philosophical Library, Inc.

15 East 40th Street, New York, N. Y.

All rights reserved

Library of Congress Catalog Card Number: 63-19700

Printed in the United States of America

338.9
F833

CONTENTS

ECONOMIC CONTROL

AND

FREE ENTERPRISE

CHAPTER I

INTRODUCTION

This book is an hypothesis on the operation of the controlled economy. For the moment it may be said that by a controlled economy is meant one that is basically the same as that of the United States of the present time, but with somewhat more systematic application of the means of control. A number of proposals concerning the nature of the control measures and the scheme of application form a part of the hypothesis.

It is believed that a number of the ideas presented in this study are novel, and it is hoped that these will merit the attention of the professional economists. It is also hoped that the analysis may help many with a non-professional interest in economics to a better understanding of how the controlled economy may be expected to operate.

In an hypothesis the individual arguments may sometimes seem insubstantial when considered by themselves; but they may take on greater stature when considered in relation to the whole thought structure. It is hoped that when the arguments do seem insubstantial, judgment will be reserved until their place in the over-all structure is clear.

In connection with an earlier work, *The Era of Continuous Prosperity,* the writer was criticized for "seeming confusion between determinant and determined." It is believed that where there are apparent inversions of the accepted order of things—or any apparent departures from notions which enjoy widespread acceptance—these are deliberate parts of the hypothesis. For these matters, too, it is asked that judgment be reserved until their place in the whole scheme of thought is clear.

At this point the writer feels called upon to explain certain aspects of the manner in which the material is arranged. Chapter II, consisting of 46 sections, is a broad outline of all the principles and proposals that constitute the hypothesis. A significant feature of this outline is that the material is arranged in depth. This is to say that an idea may be introduced briefly in one section and enlarged upon in one or more later sections. In addition, some of the material is amplified upon in the chapters following Chapter III. (Besides this, reference is made in a few places to the writer's earlier work, mentioned above, for additional discussions on the notions involved.)

Chapter III is a commentary on some views in current economic thought and their relationship to the principles in Chapter II. The general arrangement is similar to that in Chapter II.

In Chapters II and III it has been the object to make each section a self-contained entity, insofar as this was possible. For this reason, and possibly others, there is some amount of repetition or redundancy. It is believed, however, that there are few cases in which the redundancy is not attended by reference to some new facets of the matters at hand.

It is believed that there will be a tendency for some of the notions presented to be misunderstood because of a misleading resemblance to other notions, some of them held to be specious, which are in current use. In some cases careful study of the discussions will be required if misunderstandings of this kind are to be avoided.

As a related matter, it is expected that many of the discussions will be found tedious. It may be that much of the fault in this lies in the writer's limited capabilities. But it is also believed that at least a part of the explanation lies in the need for precision in differentiating the notions presented from those which have a superficial resemblance. Where the discussions seem needlessly complex or devious, it is asked that judgment be reserved, as it may be found that the treatment is justified in dealing with the niceties involved.

The writer hesitates to make specific reference to any portions of the hypothesis considered to be novel, since it is believed that this is a highly subjective matter. It is suggested, however, that a study of this kind may be novel in three general ways. First, some of the individual notions may be novel in the over-all outline. Secondly, some of the notions, though familiar in outline, may be novel with regard to the quantitative relationships involved. And thirdly, some discussions may be novel for the degree of precision with which they clarify the details of familiar notions. It is believed that a few of the ideas presented are novel in the first of these ways, and that many are novel in the latter ways.

Going a step further, and at the same time summarizing some of the earlier remarks, it is believed that portions of the hypothesis offer a new and useful style in dealing with economic problems. This is a style of thought as well as a style of writing. What is meant by this is illustrated in Section 25, wherein a concept of this hypothesis is compared with a superficially similar concept in current use. This discussion may serve better than any of the others to indicate the advantages of the style in question over the present techniques in economic thought.

One criticism that may be levelled against this style is that in striving for greater clarity it tends to oversimplify. To some extent this criticism will be valid. It is believed, however, that a more appropriate evaluation is that the treatment provides a first approximation to the truth. Like any other first approximation, it has its deficiencies. The question that must be weighed is whether or not it provides a more useful approximation to the truth than do present approaches.

It may sometimes seem that this hypothesis is intended as a blueprint for solving all of the major economic problems that may present themselves. This will be a misinterpretation. It is believed, however, that the hypothesis offers many specific proposals which should be useful in the controlled economy, and that there are implicit recommendations for the adjustment of current economic thought which should make for more profitable application to the controlled economy, and to the non-controlled economy as well.

The analyses rely to a great extent on the use of models, mainly for the sake of illustration. In connection with these there will generally be the question of how appropriate they are for the actual economy, with regard to the behavior illustrated. As has been suggested for all arguments of the hypothesis, each model case may be examined on its own merits, but it should also be judged on the manner in which it fits in with the whole structure of thought.

The remainder of this introduction is concerned with some additional comments on the arrangement of the material. The first of these relates to terms and symbols. Appendix A is a glossary of special terms and symbols and a few familiar terms. A way in which the glossary may be useful is as a reminder of special connotations associated with the terms. For example, the glossary serves as a reminder that by the aggregate demand (as defined in the text) is ordinarily meant the current rate of demand, as opposed to the volume over some period, and that ordinarily the measure is in current dollars, as opposed to constant, or adjusted, dollars.

Secondly, a note is required with regard to certain gaps that appear in the explanations of certain principles and processes, especially in connection with the models. In a number of cases the practice has been to state premises and the conclusions that derive from them, with little or no indication of the logic intervening between premises and conclusions. The reason for this is that the logic involved is so elementary in nature that it would not seem worthy of the space required in presenting it. In any such case the reader can usually verify the conclusions, if he so chooses, by assuming a set of numbers for initial conditions and carrying out the numerical processes suggested by the premises and conclusions. It is believed that scholars will find no serious errors in the logic.

Lastly, it must be said that since the analyses cover a great deal of territory, it has been necessary, for the sake of keeping the book within a reasonable length, to state some of the arguments with more succinctness than would be desirable for comfortable reading. This is especially true of the supporting arguments in the later chapters. It is believed that scholars, who are prepared to study the arguments carefully, will find them quite elementary. If professional economists find the arguments tedious, a large part of the explanation may lie in the fact that the arguments represent a new style of thought, as suggested earlier. Others, with a more casual interest in economics, may find it rewarding to follow the broader outlines of the analyses, without great concern for the supporting arguments.

CHAPTER II

The sections of this chapter outline all of the principles, notions, and proposals that comprise the hypothesis. Most of these relate only to the controlled economy. A few relate to the non-controlled economy, or to both the controlled and non-controlled economies.

SECTION 1

Scope of Control

A comprehensive definition of the controlled economy may be approached through a discussion of the scope of control. The extent to which the proposed control arrangements will penetrate into the workings of the economy may best be appreciated as the details of these arrangements are unfolded. But for an introductory view the broader features of control may be stated in this way:

*

1. A principal function of the government will be to regulate the over-all level of activity, or the aggregate demand. It may also influence the distribution of the demand to some extent, as in relieving regional hardships, but this type of activity will be of secondary importance. The principal means of regulating the aggregate demand will be fiscal and monetary practices similar to those now employed in the United States, but with some significant differences.

*

2. The government will not employ direct price and wage controls, or any other measures which may detract in similar degree from individual freedom of enterprise.

*

3. The government will take an active interest in matters of wage rates and pricing policies. In the more immediate sense its function will be to participate, as a mediator, in disputes over wage rates and pricing policies, for the sake of bringing about settlements that are reasonably equitable and conducive toward a satisfactory economic state. In a larger sense it will lead a continuing effort, engaged in by the leadership in all segments of society, toward the formulation of a code for judging the merits of any wage rate or pricing dispute. It is a part of the general hypothesis, as developed presently, that in a sense this type of activity is not vital to the workings of the controlled economy. But the well-being of the economy will improve as these efforts become more effective, and the government will be under obligation to pursue these activities in the same way that it will always be under obligation to participate in such efforts as relieving the hardships of racial discrimination.

SECTION 2

Broad Characteristics of the Controlled Economy

The characteristics which distinguish the controlled economy, as conceived of in this hypothesis, from economies which have a semblance of control, as in the case of the United States, are stated here. An economy may also be considered controlled if it has characteristics which may be recognized as being equivalent to those stated here. But any other economy will be referred to as a non-controlled economy. For the present the United States must be considered to be among the non-controlled economies. The characteristics in question are as follows:

*

1. The economy employs control devices which are quite powerful in regulating the aggregate demand. These are outlined in Section 16. These devices are similar to those now in use in the United States, but are somewhat more advanced. Perhaps the most important advance is the use of a flexible tax rate on the first income bracket, as proposed by the Commission on Money and Credit, with the understanding that the government will reduce this rate to any extent necessary in effecting upward corrections of the aggregate demand.

*

2. For each fiscal year there is a projected curve which defines the desired, or optimal, course of the aggregate demand. The manner in which this curve is established is set forth in Section 3. The government operates the controls so as to keep the actual aggregate demand as close as possible to this curve. The principle of employing a projected optimal curve in this way is, perhaps, the greatest distinction between the controlled and non-controlled economies.

*

3. It is a part of the hypothesis that the proposed means of control will enable the government to keep the actual curve of aggregate demand very close to the desired curve. The matter of how great the discrepancies may be is discussed in Section 35. For most discussions there will be no serious distortions if it be taken that the discrepancies in question are negligible.

SECTION 3

The Basic Scheme of Control

For the matters set forth in this section it is important that three terms be defined quite clearly. These are the aggregate demand, the output of the economy, and the capacity output of the economy. The aggregate demand is the demand for all goods and services, and is equal in magnitude to the gross national product. But of primary importance is that ordinarily the term implies the rate of demand in monetary measure, or current dollars per unit of time, such as current dollars per week or per year. The output of the economy is also equal in magnitude to the gross national product; but here the term ordinarily implies rate of output in *real* measure, or adjusted dollars per unit of time. (By adjusted dollars is meant what is commonly referred to as constant dollars.) The capacity output of the economy is a somewhat arbitrary entity, being the rate of output, in real measure, corresponding to full employment. It appears that there is no general agreement as to what this may be at any time. However, we shall be mainly concerned with the increase in the capacity output from year to year, and for this fairly reliable evaluations are obtainable. Thus there should be no objection to talking about the capacity output so long as the meaning of the analysis depends only on incremental values.

It is proposed, now, that the organization of the economy shall be such as to provide for these functions: (a) The desired course of the aggregate demand, as referred to in Section 2, shall be mapped by the legislature. More specifically, it is proposed that the legislature shall define the desired course of the aggregate demand for each fiscal year through advance planning, in much the same way that it establishes the budget and tax schedules for each fiscal year. (b) It is proposed that it shall be the function of the executive department to operate the controls so as to keep the actual aggregate demand as close as possible to the desired curve. In this the executive department shall be free to operate the controls as it sees fit. (This scheme was proposed by the writer in the work referred to in Chapter I.)

It is further proposed that the manner in which the legislature establishes the desired curve for any given year shall be as follows:

*

1. For the given year the desired curve will be a straight line, continuing from the desired curve up to that year, and rising by a particular percentage of the value at the point where the new segment begins.

*

2. The minimum percentage rise in the given year will be the percentage by which the capacity output of the economy is expected to rise, according to the best estimates, through increases in the work force and productivity.

*

3. The actual percentage by which the projected curve rises for the given year will be the value referred to in item 2 plus some arbitrary value, assigned at the discretion of the legislature, which will be referred to as the *planning cushion*. For example, if it is estimated that the capacity output will increase by 4 percent in the given year, and if the legislature decides upon a planning cushion of 1 percent, the desired curve for the given year will rise by 5 percent of the value at the beginning of the year.

*

4. If as the given year progresses it becomes apparent that the rise in productive capacity is significantly different from the estimated value, the executive department will be empowered to alter the desired curve to correct for this discrepancy.

SECTION 4

Purpose of the Proposed Scheme

Aside from the fact that the scheme just outlined will provide for systematic application of the means of control, it is argued that this scheme will be of great importance in dealing with the forces of inflation that are bound to occur in the controlled economy. The principles involved are stated briefly at this point and are discussed at greater length in Chapter V.

Before proceeding it should be said that by inflation is meant any rise of the price index applying to the gross national product. The rate of inflation is the rate of rise of the price index, and it will always be implicit that this is in percent per year.

It is held that whenever there is a state of full employment, or a close approach to full employment, there will be strong inflationary pressures present, because of the natural tendencies of labor and business, under this state, in seeking the highest possible wage rates and profit margins. Because of this it will generally be necessary to maintain a compromise state under which some sizable percentage of unemployment exists as a buffer to the forces of inflation, but under which some moderate rate of inflation is tolerated in the interest of making unemployment lower than it would be under a perfectly stable price index. There will naturally be a great deal of dissatisfaction with the unemployment that exists; but there will also be a great deal of dissatisfaction with the continuous rise of prices. The state that is maintained must strike a balance between these two evils. The government cannot set out to maintain full employment no matter how rapidly prices may advance, nor can it set out to maintain a perfectly stable price index no matter how employment may suffer under this state. There must be a compromise in these matters, and the compromise must be one that meets with the approval of the electorate. The proposed scheme will be an instrumentality through which a compromise satisfactory to the electorate is arrived at in a systematic way.

As is discussed in Chapter V, the key to the compromise between inflation and unemployment will lie in the choice of the planning cushion. In a sense the choice of the planning cushion will be the most important discretionary decision of the economy. What follows here is an abstract of the discussions in Chapter V on the influence of the planning cushion.

First, it may be said that this rule applies: (a) If over the long period the rate of inflation consistently exceeds the planning cushion, the percentage of unemployment will rise; and the percentage of unemployment will fall if the rate of inflation is consistently less than the planning cushion. (b) If a constant planning cushion is maintained over the long period, the rate of inflation will stabilize at a value equal to the planning cushion, and the percentage of unemployment will stabilize at a level commensurate with the planning cushion, or rate of inflation.

How the planning cushion influences the behavior of the economy is illustrated in these cases:

*

1. Let it be supposed that over some long period the planning cushion is held at 2 percent. The hypothesis holds that in the long run inflation will proceed fairly steadily at a mean rate of 2 percent per year, and that unemployment will remain fairly steady at some level commensurate with the given rate of inflation, such as 4 percent of the work force.

*

2. Proceeding from the state of affairs in case 1, let it be supposed that there is widespread dissatisfaction with the level of unemployment. A remedy will lie in liberalizing the planning cushion, causing the aggregate demand to rise more rapidly. Let it be supposed, then, that the planning cushion is raised to 3 percent, and held at this value over the long period. In the long run the rate of inflation will have a mean value of 3 percent per year, and unemployment will steady out at a value lower than in case 1, such as 3 percent of the work force.

*

3. Proceeding once more from the state of affairs in case 1, let it be supposed that there is widespread dissatisfaction with the rate of inflation. A remedy will lie in reducing the planning cushion. Let it be supposed, then, that the planning cushion is reduced to nil, and held at that value over the long period. Here the mean rate of inflation will be nil in the long run, but unemployment will steady out at a value higher that in case 1, such as 7 percent of the work force.

*

These cases illustrate how the compromise between inflation and unemployment is crystallized in the choice of the planning cushion. A high planning cushion makes for a state of indulgence — one in which unemployment is low and inflation is rapid. A low planning cushion makes for a state of austerity — relatively high unemployment and fairly stable prices.

Since the compromise must be determined in accordance with the wishes of the electorate — they will be the ultimate authority as to what constitutes a satisfactory compromise — it would seem appropriate to have the value of the planning cushion decided by the legislature, as in the proposed arrangement. However, as an alternative to the proposed arrangement, it might prove satisfactory to have the executive department choose the planning cushion. This would mean, simply, that the executive would be responsible to the electorate for maintaining a suitable compromise between inflation and unemployment, instead of the legislature.

But it is submitted that whether basic policy is chosen by the legislature or the executive, the kind of definition that would obtain under the proposed scheme would be a big step forward. It is submitted that by contrast the present arrangement in the United States — which consists, it appears, of "applying the brakes" whenever the forces of inflation are more conspicuous than the effects of unemployment, and "opening the throttle" when the situation is reversed — is quite unsatisfactory. The fault is not in opening the throttle and applying the brakes as the occasion demands. The fault is in not having clear-cut criteria for directing these operations — criteria which give due weight to the balance between inflation and unemployment, and which are sufficiently meaningful to the people to enable them to have an intelligent voice in the determination of policy.

SECTION 5

Government Management versus Inflation

It is sometimes believed that full employment and a perfectly stable (constant) price index can co-exist if only government fiscal and monetary policies are sound according to traditional standards. It is held that this view is erroneous and that it interferes with a sensible approach to the problem of fighting inflation.

Given that a state of full, or nearly full, employment exists, with the aggregate demand at the level necessary to sustain this level of employment, this factor alone produces severe inflationary pressures, no matter what the current fiscal and monetary practices may be. These pressures, generally referred to as cost-push pressures, and referred to in this hypothesis as cost-profit-push pressures, are due to the efforts of labor in seeking the highest possible wage rates, and of business in seeking the highest possible profit margins. The most direct process by which these pressures are eased is by a reduction in the level of employment. (An indirect process is moral suasion, as considered presently.) But if we are given that the aggregate demand remains high enough to maintain full, or nearly full, employment, then the inflationary pressures will remain unchanged no matter how the fiscal and monetary policies responsible for the given level of aggregate demand are altered. In seeking the highest possible wage rates and profit margins labor and business know only that a prosperous state exists and that this is favorable to their ventures; they are in no way influenced by the fiscal and monetary practices that serve to provide the prosperous state.

While the more conservative economists believe that traditionally unsound practices are responsible for the cost-profit-push pressures attending a high level of employment, some less conservative economists believe that certain traditionally unsound courses are less inflationary than others. For example, one belief among the latter economists is that if deficit financing is required to increase the aggregate demand by a given amount, for the sake of reducing unemployment, it will be less inflationary if the goverment bonds are sold to the general public rather than to the banks. It is held that the outlook comprised by beliefs of this kind is erroneous and retrogressive. It is futile to try to avoid the cost-profit-push inflationary pressures by juggling fiscal and monetary policies where these are intended to bring about a given rise in the aggregate demand. Where a given rise of aggregate demand is required to bring about a desired decrease in unemployment, any course of action that brings about the required rise in aggregate demand will be greeted with the same increase in the cost-profit-push inflationary pressures as any other course that may be followed.

It is held, too, that when society comes to a better understanding of this principle, it will be in a far better position to attack the problem of inflation through more hopeful means. These include, first, the course of systematic compromise between inflation and unemployment, and, secondly, moral suasion, as discussed below.

SECTION 6

Moral Suasion

The principle just stated may be paraphrased by saying that inflation and a high level of employment are bound together by ties which cannot be weakened by manipulation of fiscal and monetary policies. More generally it may be said that there are no mechanistic means, short of measures in the class of direct price controls, by which these ties can be weakened. However, it is possible that a humanistic approach, which may be referred to as moral suasion, will accomplish in some measure what the mechanistic means cannot.

Specifically, the object of moral suasion will be to make the cost-profit-push pressures lower for any given level of employment than they would be in the absence of this influence. If moral suasion is successful in this, then for any rate of inflation that is tolerated, as part of the compromise between inflation and unemployment, the percentage of unemployment will be lower than it would otherwise be.

In the broadest view moral suasion must include three lines of endeavor: (1) There must be a continuing campaign, waged by the leadership in all sectors of society, for moderation on the part of labor and business in their quests for higher wage rates and profit margins. (2) There must be a continuing effort by the leadership to develop a code by which society may be guided in judging the merits in any dispute over wage rates and pricing policy. At an early stage of development, as in the United States at the present time, this code will be a relatively poor guide, and society will have to proceed largely upon its intuition, as unsatisfactory as this may be. It is not to be expected that the code will ever provide clear-cut formulas, although it sometimes may, and it is a part of the concept that the code will not have legal status (if any parts become law they will cease to be part of the code); but as the code takes on definition, and as it gains in popular acceptance, the campaign of moral suasion will become increasingly effective. (3) It will be important for the well-being of society, and for the success of the campaign of moral suasion, that the planning cushion be stable over the long period — in the sense of changing slowly — so as to make for a stable compromise between inflation and unemployment; and it will devolve upon the leadership to guide the people in maintaining this kind of stability. Without this kind of leadership the demands of the people may bring about oscillations in policy between extreme indulgence and extreme austerity, each extreme occurring as a reaction from the other. Both extremes will be unsatisfactory to the people, and capable leadership can guide them to a stable mean.

It is a popular notion that moral suasion is doomed to failure because of the "perversities of human nature." It may be that this is so. But in any case a reasonable course of action for the economy will be to proceed with the scheme of compromise between inflation and unemployment, through choice of the planning cushion, and to try to make moral suasion work. It is possible that when the importance of moral suasion is realized, efforts along these lines will take on the character of a social cause — like that of relieving interracial difficulties — and under this kind of spirit progress may be surprisingly rapid.

It appears that much of the apathy attending the approach of moral suasion may be a by-product of impatience to proceed along a more direct line of action, as along the line of price controls. The objections to price controls may be summed up by saying that this course is inconsistent with freedom of enterprise. But this is only a short way of saying that there are enormous difficulties in setting up a system of price controls that will provide for a generally satisfactory state; and until these difficulties can be overcome the evils of price controls are almost certain to be far greater than those which the price controls are expected to eliminate. The evidence of this is to be found in the experience of the United States during World War II, and in the experience of the USSR.

If it is possible that a workable system of price controls can be developed, the most painless way of developing this system should be through the approach of developing a code of ethics of the kind referred to in item (2) above. That is, if there is merit in price controls, this should become apparent as the code of ethics develops, and the system of price controls should be the natural culmination of the code of ethics. But, on the other hand, if there is little merit in price controls, because of insurmountable difficulties, this too should be apparent in the evolutionary process and should enable society to steer clear of these difficulties.

Another direct approach in the class of price controls is compulsory arbitration in wage disputes. Here too standards are required, for guiding the arbitrators, and if there is merit in this scheme it should emerge as an evolutionary by-product of the development of the code of ethics.

SECTION 7

Another View of Inflation

Another view of the inflationary pressures is one in which any rise of the price index is entirely a function of how wage rates behave. For an approximate analysis this view is quite meaningful and useful. The principles involved are outlined briefly at this point and discussed at greater length in Chapter V.

The basis for the view in question is the principle that the return of labor as a whole tends to remain very close to a fixed percentage of the aggregate demand, as discussed in *A Law That Cannot Be Repealed, Challenge, April 1962.* Implicit in this is that profits as a whole tend to remain close to a fixed markup on labor costs. As is discussed in Chapter V, this tendency leads to certain conclusions, which are approximately correct, as follows: (1) If on the average wage rates rise proportionately with productivity, the price index will remain constant. (2) If wage rates rise less rapidly than productivity, the price index will fall, and if they rise more rapidly, the price index will rise.

These principles provide a clear view of the mechanics by which the inflationary pressures fall off as the percentage of unemployment increases. As unemployment increases, the demands of labor become less insistent, and the mean rate at which wage rates rise tapers off. When the rate of rise of wages has tapered off to the point where it matches the rate of rise of productivity, the rise of the price index ceases.

SECTION 8

On Freedom of Enterprise

An underlying view of this hypothesis is that the system of controls proposed is consistent with reasonable notions of free enterprise. Naturally this view is highly subjective and may meet with much opposition that is rational. But it is suggested that control is not categorically the antithesis of freedom, and that if the proposed control arrangements are to be attacked as detracting from individual freedom, they must be attacked on their merits rather than on the basis that they do impose control.

The view of freedom subscribed to here is substantially the same as that stated by Woodrow Wilson in *The New Freedom*. The basic argument in that discourse is that constraints and disciplines form a matrix without which the freedoms we value could not exist. In a nutshell, this is to say that freedom must not be confused with dissoluteness.

An analogy that may serve to illustrate this principle is afforded by the function of a traffic light at a busy intersection. In one sense the traffic light detracts from freedom, since no one may legally proceed against the stop signal. But in another sense it contributes toward freedom by minimizing traffic snarls and making the flow of traffic more orderly and convenient than it would be with no traffic light. To anyone who has seen the intersection only at times of sparse traffic the signal light may seem a senseless curtailment of freedom. But to those who are acquainted with the difficulties during times of heavy traffic the signal light is a source of freedom.

A principle illustrated by this analogy is that freedom is never absolute. In any situation we must choose from various types of constraint, and in so doing we choose from various types of freedom. Another lesson — repeated in all the laws by which civilized man lives — is that the freedoms occurring in any area under governmental regulation are generally more desirable than those that would occur in the absence of this regulation.

Whether any given proposal for governmental control in economic affairs will detract from or add to the cause of individual freedom of enterprise must be a matter of individual judgment, and in a democracy must ultimately be decided by the electorate. But it is a great abuse of intellect to hold that control and freedom of enterprise must be mutually exclusive.

SECTION 9

Government Neutrality

In an extreme view government neutrality, or laissez-faire, implies complete dissociation of the government from economic affairs. It makes as little sense, however, to think of a state of this kind as it does to think of a pound of flesh without any blood in it. When this view is set aside, all other notions of laissez-faire become quite indistinct, like notions of fairness between labor and employers. It is the purpose at this point to suggest a concept of laissez-faire, or neutrality, which may serve as a standard for the controlled economy, and which may be extended, as well, to the non-controlled economy.

It is suggested that a particular state in the controlled economy may be taken as a standard of this kind. This is the state that obtains when the planning cushion is kept at nil over the long period. This standard will not apply to individual policies of the government, but it will apply to the summation, or net effect, of all policies.

It may seem incongruous to speak of laissez-faire in the controlled economy, just as it may seem incongruous to believe that freedom of enterprise can flourish as vigorously under control as under the lack of it. But a simple analogy may serve to illustrate the logic of the opposite view. In this analogy one man stands on shore and quietly watches another man drown nearby. A life preserver lies close at hand, and might be effective in a rescue attempt; also help is within calling distance; but the man on shore disdains to intervene in any way. To some this behavior may seem a model of neutrality, or laissez-faire. Yet by reasonable standards it comes closer to manslaughter than it does to neutrality. By rcasonable standards the man on shore is under obligation to perform certain minimum services, such as throwing the life preserver and calling for help; and only after he has performed these minimum services can his behavior be considered neutral. Doing nothing cannot be taken as a standard of neutrality in this case; and in the same way doing nothing cannot be taken as a standard of neutrality for government behavior in economic affairs.

If government neutrality is to have any sensible meaning at all, it must be as something other than non-intervention. It might be well if words such as laissez-faire, welfare state, free market economy, and government coddling were not used at all in discussing economic affairs. But these words do play a large part in political argument, and because of this it would seem well to have a reasonable datum of government neutrality.

To see why the state under a nil planning cushion suggests itself as one of government neutrality in economic affairs, let it be supposed that to begin with the planning cushion is some fairly large value, such as 3 percent, over the long period. In the long run this will bring about a steady inflation at a mean rate of 3 percent per year as indicated in Section 4. This will be objectionable in many quarters, and from the conservative point of view — to which deference is made in defining neutrality — this will be characteristic of the welfare state, since the only reason for the objectionable inflation will be that of making unemployment lower than it would be with a nil planning cushion.

A question that now arises is this: How far must the government retreat from its policy of indulgence to overcome the objections of the conservatives? The answer proposed is that it need retreat only to the point where the planning cushion is nil, since in the long run this will make for a perfectly stable price index. A second question is: What purpose would be served by retreating to a negative planning cushion? The answer here is that this policy would be deflationary in the long run and would depress employment in a way that could not be justified on any reasonable basis. If we grant that a positive planning cushion is characteristic of the welfare state, by reason of reducing unemployment at the expense of a steady inflation, then by this judgment we determine that the negative planning cushion is anti-welfare, by reason of sacrificing employment for no more useful purpose than bringing about a deflation. Thus the nil planning cushion represents neutrality in the sense that it stands at the dividing line between what may be considered government indulgence and what must be considered senseless oppression.

On the other hand — from the more liberal point of view — if maintaining a nil planning cushion is to be considered a neutral policy, it must provide the people with the opportunity for maintaining a satisfactory level of employment. Given that the economy has maintained a nil planning cushion, and that unemployment has been fairly high, say 7 percent of the work force, the question arises as to whether or not unemployment can be reduced under the continuation of a nil planning cushion. The answer is that if the people suppress the inflationary tendencies to the point where the price index falls, this will, in time, lead to an improvement in employment. (This follows from the rule stated in Section 4 on the planning cushion versus the rate of inflation. Also, as indicated in Section 7, it is not required that wage rates fall, but only that they rise less rapidly, on the average, than productivity. And the improvement in employment will continue as long as the price index continues to fall.) Thus the people do have it in their power to provide and maintain a satisfactory level of employment under a nil planning cushion. It will, of course, be far more difficult to do so than under some moderate positive planning cushion.

It is not proposed in this hypothesis that the economy should be bound to a policy of neutrality in the sense just defined. It is probable that the electorate will generally prefer a policy that leans in the direction of the welfare state. But if the conservative element should prevail upon the electorate to choose the course of neutrality — it appears that it will be a long time before they cease trying to do so — then the course of action should be that of maintaining a nil planning cushion. To maintain a nil planning cushion will be to allow labor and business to "stew in their own juice." This is to say that through suitable self-discipline in suppressing the inflationary tendencies they may maintain a satisfactory level of employment, and wantonness will lead to an unsatisfactory level of employment. But to make the planning cushion negative will be to spike the juice with carbolic acid.

For the sake of comparing this concept of neutrality with the conservative notions of laissez-faire, let it be supposed that a given non-controlled economy is managed in a way that goes quite far in honoring these latter notions. Also, let it be supposed that over some period this policy causes the economy to behave in a manner parallel to that of a controlled economy with a negative planning cushion. For example, let it be supposed that in a given year the capacity output of the economy rises by 3 percent but that the aggregate demand remains constant. In this case the economy behaves in the same way as a controlled economy with a planning cushion of minus 3 percent, and we may say that the economy has an *effective* planning cushion for that year of minus 3 percent. It is held that this is oppressive to the people and unworthy of a modern government. It is the concept that in this case the government is no more neutral than the unconcerned man in the analogy stated earlier. Just as it is not neutral for this man to do nothing, so is it not neutral for the government to follow the traditional notions of neutrality simply because these keep government intervention to a minimum. The concept is that policy should be considered neutral in the non-controlled economy only if it leads to a nil effective planning cushion.

Perhaps the greatest fault with the traditional notions of laissez-faire lies in trying to evaluate individual components of policy. It is held that no component of policy, such as maintaining a balanced budget, can be considered neutral simply because it smacks of a minimum of government intervention; some other standard is required. The question, then, is what shall the standard be. The answer proposed here is that it is futile to try to find standards of neutrality for individual components of policy. We must be content with standards for over-all policy, such as those suggested — a nil planning cushion for the controlled economy, and a nil effective planning cushion for the non-controlled economy.

Whether or not the proposed standards are reasonable is a matter of taste. It is possible that other, more appealing standards may be found. But it is suggested that these must not be based on non-intervention, and that they should be at least as specific as those proposed.

SECTION 10

ALIGNMENT OF THE DEMAND

Alignment of the demand will be a short way of saying: the degree of correspondence between the manner in which the aggregate demand is distributed and the manner in which productive capabilities are oriented. If the alignment is unsatisfactory, correction may come about either through a change in the distribution of the demand or through a change in the orientation of productive capabilities, as through a shift of labor from the more backward sectors of the economy to the more active ones.

The maintenance of a satisfactory level of employment requires both a satisfactory magnitude of aggregate demand and a satisfactory alignment of the demand. It is a part of the hypothesis, however, that in the controlled economy the government will not be required to intervene in any large measure in the matter of alignment. It should be adequate if the government maintains the optimal magnitude of aggregate demand by means which do not obtrude on the alignment of the demand. One such means, for example, is a flexible tax rate on the first income bracket. But the government may at times employ public works projects, and possibly other means, to relieve severe distress in the more stubbornly backward sectors.

Also, it should be helpful if the government maintains a program for training labor in preparation for transfer to new employment, and for providing other financial support in facilitating such transfers.

The degree to which the demand remains aligned with productive capabilities will depend upon such things as the stability of the distribution of the demand (tastes of the people), the flexibility of industry in adjusting to changes in distribution of the demand, displacement of labor by automation, and the mobility of labor. It is a basic tenet of the hypothesis that if the aggregate demand is always kept at a suitably high level, the flexibility of industry and the mobility of labor will be adequate to offset the disruptive influences of automation and shifts in the distribution of the demand. The theory is that, with the aggregate demand held at the optimal level, there will always be many sectors of the economy operating at a brisk pace, and these sectors will provide ample opportunities for the transfer of labor to them from the backward sectors.

Those who oppose this theory will hold up to view the apparent contradictions in the non-controlled economy. It is significant, however, that automation and the immobility of labor loom as great problems in times of recession or depression, or when the demand in most sectors of the economy is slack, and that they fade into the background when things are booming in most sectors. It is held that the experience of the United States in periods of generally slack demand, as in the past few years, is not in any way an index of the mobility of labor under a continuously prosperous state.

Some facets of the matter may be examined more closely by considering, for study purposes, a somewhat unrealistic model case as follows: (1) The prices of all goods and services are fixed. (2) The economy is self-subsistent; there is no foreign trade. (3) Control has just been adopted, and employment stands at 90 percent of the work force. (4) The government proceeds to raise the aggregate demand in order to bring employment up to a satisfactory level.

In this case these developments may be expected: (a) As the aggregate demand rises, certain industries or sectors of the economy will reach a volume of production equal to nominal capacity and then will be required to expand production through overtime work schedules. As the demand continues to rise, more and more sectors will find themselves in this position. (b) Some sectors of the economy will lag behind the general rise to an extent that will permit a large amount of unemployment to persist in these sectors. (c) At some point — possibly when employment is in the region of 98 percent — the government will find it expedient to bring the rise in demand to a halt. At this point the volume of overtime work will be quite heavy in many sectors, and the difficulties in relocating workers from the backward sectors to the busier ones will be so great as to make further increases in the demand of little value. (d) With many sectors operating on heavy overtime work schedules, conditions will be favorable for the relocation of workers from the backward sectors, and in time employment may come very close to 100 percent.

To make the model more appropriate for the actual economy, let it now be supposed that prices are free to vary. Here the difficulties in maintaining a satisfactory alignment of the demand are increased by the inflationary pressures that attend a prosperous state. As the aggregate demand rises and overtime work schedules begin to appear in force, the inflationary pressures developing will make it necessary for the government to bring the rise in aggregate demand to a halt at an earlier point than would be possible in the absence of inflationary pressures. This means that there will be fewer sectors working on overtime schedules than would otherwise be the case, and fewer sectors working very close to capacity; and therefore conditions will be less conducive to the relocation of labor from the lagging sectors. But on the other hand conditions will become more favorable for the transfer of labor from the lagging sectors as moral suasion becomes more effective in suppressing the inflationary pressures. With increasing cooperation from labor and business in checking the inflationary pressures, it will be possible for the government to increase the number of sectors operating at or above capacity.

Passing from these qualitative observations, this quantitative speculation is offered for the United States, assuming that control is adopted: At any time some volume of unemployment must be present as a buffer to the forces of inflation. The experience of the United States, especially in the last decade, indicates that it will be difficult to reduce this volume below 4 percent of the work force, without excessive inflation, even with a vigorous campaign of moral suasion; and 2 percent of unemployment seems to be the most optimistic goal within reason. It is speculated that if it should be possible to check the inflationary pressures so that these do not stand in the way of bringing unemployment down to the level of 2 percent, then difficulties connected with the alignment of the demand will not stand in the way of this achievement either.

One of the views of classical economics is that price rises must precede an expansion of capacity in the busier sectors of the economy, the price rises acting as an inducement to expansion. It is suggested that this view is highly academic and inappropriate for the actual economy. In the first place the presence of persistent overtime work schedules, without price increases, is as strong an incentive to increases in capacity as could be wanted. Secondly, where industries are operating at close to capacity on a sustained basis, it is a general policy of management to pursue expansion activities in anticipation of future increases in demand. It is true that where industries experience brisk demand there is a tendency for management to take advantage of the situation by raising prices. This is a part of the cost-profit-push phenomena. But it cannot be said that this is a necessary part of the mechanics of the economy. Management should meet excessive demand with overtime production without price increases, and the campaign of moral suasion should aim at promoting this type of behavior. Where the demand is so great that it cannot be met through overtime work schedules, the government should apply sales taxes to reduce the demand (the demand in this case being the monies applying for goods and services after taxes), in order to preserve orderly marketing conditions.

Foreign trade will be a factor of some importance in the alignment of the demand. This is discussed in Sections 13 and 14. At this point, however, it may be said that foreign trade can be a means for improving the alignment of the demand, or its effects can be adverse. The principal aim in international negotiations on foreign trade agreements should be improvement of the alignment of the demand for the several nations. This will be of especially great importance for some of the smaller nations. Under the present arrangements the problem of arriving at the best distribution of world trade is complicated by the problems connected with balances of payments. Under an arrangement proposed in Section 13, these problems are separated from each other, and the nations may negotiate more freely on the matter of the most beneficial distribution of world trade without having their negotiations trammelled by considerations for arriving at satisfactory balances of payments.

SECTION 11

AUTOMATION

Automation is just one phase of technological progress. Yet in the popular concept automation looms so large as to constitute the bulk of technological progress, and the discussions at this point will defer to this concept.

The views of this hypothesis on automation in the controlled economy are summarized by the following observations:

*

1. Subject to certain qualifications, this generalization may be made: In the controlled economy the people will strive to produce as much goods and services as they possibly can. The government will regulate the aggregate demand so that all the goods and services produced are absorbed by the people. The economy will welcome rapid advances in automation. These contribute toward increasing the total amount of goods and services that can be produced, and thus increase each person's real return, or the standard of living. In a practical sense automation is the only source from which increases in the standard of living derive. To believe that automation may lead to overproduction in an economy such as the United States is to believe that the people cannot use a vastly higher standard of living than now exists. This is nonsense. It is sometimes held that the economy must find new products for consumption to offset the effects of automation. The view here is that for practical purposes the potential demand for existing types of goods and services may be regarded as limitless.

To see that this is so we have only to go down the list of existing types of goods and services and consider how close the people of the United States are to the point of complete satiety. We may consider, for example, such items as housing, household furnishings, public schools, commodious public transportation—as opposed, say, to the type of subway and bus service now available in New York City—roads, automobile parking facilities in congested areas, and adequate hospital and nursing services for all the charity cases now receiving such scant attention. Public facilities, such as schools and roads and charitable institutions, require taxes and charitable contributions in vastly greater amounts than are now forthcoming for these purposes. Taxes and contributions for these purposes are pinched because the taxpayers and donors feel they cannot afford to divert more funds from the goods and services they buy directly out of their incomes. It will be a sign of satiety among the people when there is no difficulty in levying taxes for all the public facilities we feel we need, and when charitable institutions find so little difficulty in raising funds that their problem is not in acquiring funds but rather in finding the necessary personnel for carrying out their missions. A more direct sign, of course, will be that which obtains when workers show little interest in wage increases, or give clear indications that they are channelling the bulk of their increases in real incomes into savings of muney and securities.

Reflection will show that at the present time economics is as much a study of the most beneficial use of scarce means as it was in the days of Adam Smith. In view of the scarcities that exist, it is difficult to find any justification for the view, held by so many seemingly responsible people, that because of automation the United States can now produce more goods and services than the people can possibly use.

If the economy is to operate at capacity, it is necessary, of course, that the people have the purchasing power required to absorb the capacity output. In the controlled economy the government will see to it that the people do have the needed purchasing power.

*

2. One significant qualification to the observations in item 1 is that the economy will not always operate at full capacity, but rather at a level that is near capacity. The principal reason for this is the need for maintaining some appreciable volume of unemployment as a buffer to the forces of inflation.

*

3. Another factor contributing to unemployment will be imperfect mobility of labor. In many cases the initial effect of automation is to displace labor. When the aggregate demand is regulated properly, conditions will be conducive to the re-employment of the displaced labor in other sectors of the economy. In many cases a considerable amount of time and governmental effort may be required in assisting displaced labor to prepare for employment in other sectors. Therefore there will always be some volume of unemployment attributable to the effects of automation. But it is held unlikely that this component of unemployment will make the total volume greater than it would be if there were no unemployment attributable to automation. Some volume of unemployment will be found a necessary condition for the sake of avoiding excessive inflation. This may generally be in the region of 3 percent of the work force. It is probable that the volume of unemployment attributable to automation will generally be much less than 3 percent of the work force, and that this volume will simply constitute one component of the total unemployment that must be present as a normal part of the operations of the economy.

It is held that the experience of the non-controlled economy has led to a false impression of the difficulties brought on by automation. People judge these difficulties by what they see in times of generally slack demand, as in the United States in the past few years. But this is bound to lead to a seriously distorted view. It is only natural that in such times the obstacles to the re-employment of labor displaced by automation should be much greater than they would be with brisk demand in most industries. Another factor contributing to the difficulties in the non-controlled economy is that even when things are booming, the transfer of labor from the backward sectors to the busier ones will be slower than it might be, because of the uncertainty over how long the boom will continue. In the controlled economy conditions will be conducive to greater mobility of labor not only because of the brisk demand in most sectors at any time, but also because of the assurance that the attractive conditions in these sectors will have a relatively high degree of stability.

*

4. A factor of importance in connection with automation is the length of the standard work week. Assuming for the moment that there is no technological progress of any kind, the standard of living of the people will rise or fall as the length of the work week increases or decreases. If the people work longer hours, the economy will produce more goods and services, and the real income of each person will increase. If the people work shorter hours, the reverse is true. The people must decide what the length of the standard work week should be. In effect they must strike a balance between the standard of living and the amount of leisure time they are to have. If the people in the United States were to change from the present 40 hour week to a 48 hour week, the standard of living would rise with this change, but at the sacrifice of leisure time. It is not likely that the people will elect to increase the standard work week in this way, and if the people did go so far as to take this step, there would then be great resistance to any further increases in the work week. It is for this reason that in item 1, above, it was observed that from a practical standpoint automation is the only source of increases in the standard of living.

If the people were to reduce the work week below the present level of 40 hours, this would contribute to a decrease in the standard of living. It is sometimes held that the displacement of labor through automation must be answered with a reduction of the work week. This is a foolish outlook. Reducing the work week offsets the benefits of automation, and if this outlook were allowed to hold sway, improvements in the standard of living might come to a complete standstill. The people should resist reductions in the work week until they are willing to accept a lower standard of living in exchange for more leisure time. It does not seem that at present the people are ready to make an exchange of this kind. Those who favor a reduction of the work week are under the mistaken impression that this is necessary for maintaining a satisfactory level of employment, and are not aware of the implications regarding a lower standard of living.

Arguments relating to reduction of the work week stated in terms of monetary returns are misleading. These who favor a reduction of the work week claim that it would be possible for business to reduce the work week and at the same time raise wage rates so that the take-home pay of the worker would not diminish. But any view that labor will not suffer a reduction in the standard of living must be false. If the work week is reduced, the output of the economy must fall correspondingly, and the real return of each person must therefore fall. If labor did receive the same take-home pay after a reduction of the work week, employers would be forced to raice prices, and it would be on account of the increases in prices that labor would suffer a reduction in real incomes.

SECTION 12

Growth Rate

In the controlled economy the government can proceed along two general courses in seeking to increase the growth rate. On the one hand it can lead business toward greater efficiency, through such means as research and educational programs. The object in this course is to achieve greater production without calling upon the people for any sacrifices of considerable magnitude. In the other course the government employs means which do require appreciable sacrifices. For example, subsidies on investment, either as direct grants or in the form of tax concessions, impose an additional burden of taxes on the general public, and make for a lower rate of consumption.

So long as the government employs only the first type of measure, it will be considered in this hypothesis that the growth rate is normal. But when a higher growth rate is achieved through measures entailing some kind of sacrifice, this will be referred to as an accelerated growth rate.

In the controlled economy an accelerated growth rate will be a matter entirely apart from that of maintaining a prosperous state. In the absence of special measures relating to the growth rate, the aggregate demand will always be a value which serves to keep employment at the highest level consistent with reasonable stability of prices. The limiting factor on the level of employment will be only the strength of the inflationary pressures, and what this is at any time will be independent of the growth rate. Thus it is not to be thought that an accelerated growth rate is needed for maintaining a satisfactory level of employment, or that it will in any way contribute to making employment any better than it would be with a normal growth rate.

The principal concern in connection with an accelerated growth rate will be national security, or political ascendency in world affairs. But at the same time it must be recognized that while a higher growth rate will entail a lower rate of present consumption, it will in the long run yield rewards that compensate handsomely for current sacrifices.

In promoting an accelerated growth rate the government must give attention to two factors. On the one hand it must seek to increase the tendency toward investment. But on the other hand it must also give attention to the matter of increasing the tendency toward saving (in all forms of wealth), or to some alternative as discussed below and in Section 30.

It appears likely that promoting an increase in the tendency toward saving will be a more formidable problem than increasing the tendency toward investment. This speculation is strongly represented in the study of Dr. Simon Kuznets, *Capital in the American Economy: Its Formation and Financing*. Special measures may be required in dealing with this problem.

It is held that if the government simply proceeds along the course of issuing subsidies on investment, this will lead to the necessary increase in savings, along with the desired increase in investment; but the burden of the subsidies required for a nominal increase in investment, or savings, may be one that is quite difficult for the taxpayers to bear. More specifically, it is held possible that the taxes required will be much greater than the increase in investment, possibly many times as great. (This is discussed further in Section 30.)

But there is another course that may prove to be less burdensome. This course, passed over rather lightly in the treatment of Dr. Kuznets, is one of maintaining a budgetary surplus. Under this course it is likely that the additional taxes required for a given increase in investment will be only fractionally greater than the increase in investment. (This too is discussed in Section 30.)

But no matter what course is chosen, the people will have to bear an increased tax burden, and the people will have to decide how large a sacrifice they are willing to make in the interest of greater national security or greater future returns.

A theme in the study of Dr. Kuznets is that growth in the United States is likely to be much slower in future decades than it has been in the past, and that this will generate inflationary tendencies. The concept appears to embrace the notion of a shortage of goods and services, on account of a lag in productive facilities, with the inflationary pressures developing from this shortage.

The argument in this hypothesis is that any such notion constitutes loose and specious thinking. In a sense there always has been and always will be a shortage of goods and services; for at any time in the past the people could have used more goods and services than were produced, and this relationship must, reasonably, continue through the foreseeable future. But a more sensible view — for the controlled economy at least — is that at any time the rate of output will be close to the capacity level, and the aggregate demand will be at the value necessary to absorb this output. Then there may be a shortage of goods and services in relation to dreams of what we could have had if investment had proceeded at a higher rate, but there will not be a shortage in relation to the demand.

At any time the inflationary forces are a function of how the demand is regulated, together with the moral pressures exerted in suppressing these forces. They are not a function of what might have been under a different history of capital growth.

In his study Dr. Kuznets indicates that he does not believe the people will choose to operate with a budgetary deficit. He does indicate the desirability of a change in the tax distribution to favor individuals more prone to save. This implies a shift in taxes from those individuals in the higher income brackets (including corporations) to those in the lower brackets. It seems quite plain that under this scheme a given increase in the rate of savings, or investment, will require a shift in taxes of considerably larger amount, possibly many times as much. Under the scheme of a budgetary surplus the increase in the taxes—spread in the customary way—is likely to be comparable to the increase in investment. It is difficult to see, therefore, why there is more hope of inducing the people to submit to a shift in taxes of the type suggested than of inducing them to submit to a budgetary surplus. (This is discussed at length in Section 30.)

SECTION 13

International Trade

The term international trade is used very loosely here to embrace all transactions entering into the balance of payments. It is believed that there should be no confusion as a result of this departure from the purer usage.

Because of the manner in which international trade tends to interfere with domestic control policy, it is important that this be dealt with before proceeding to the outline of domestic policy.

Proposed here is a scheme of control over international trade, to be superimposed on the present international trade arrangements, which is believed to be novel. The proposed system has two purposes. The first of these is to provide a reasonably straightforward means of overcoming the problem of troublesome deficits in international balances of payments. The second is to separate the problem of balances of payments from the problem of working out constructive world trade relationships.

The proposed arrangement would appear as a modification to existing international agreements, including GATT and that covering the organization of the IMF. Moreover the arrangement is such that it might properly be administered by the IMF under rules similar to those governing the present functions of the IMF.

It is commonly recognized that it is desirable for the balance of payments in each nation to be neutral (no surplus or deficit). That is, the balance should be neutral in the long period and it should not stray too far from neutral in the shorter periods. When the principles of domestic control are more fully understood, the desirability of neutral balances will be even plainer than it is now. It is sometimes thought that a balance-of-payments surplus is desirable for the sake of promoting prosperity, and this thought is sometimes valid for the non-controlled economy. But in the controlled economy prosperity does not depend upon a surplus in the balance of payments. Beyond this, it may be said that a surplus is a distinct disadvantage, since under it there are less goods and services available for distribution among the people at home than there would be with no surplus. A deficit in the balance of payments might be desirable for the sake of more goods and services at home, but no nation can afford a deficit for any great length of time because of the drain on the monetary means of payment. The fact that no nation should want either a surplus or a deficit in the balance of payments should be conducive to cooperation among the nations in eliminating surpluses and deficits for all.

It is commonly recognized that flexible exchange rates among the currencies of the nations, properly administered, would act in a very positive manner to preserve neutral balances of payments in all nations. (By flexible exchange rates is meant either freely varying rates on the open market or rates fixed by the governments but adjusted frequently in accordance with the demands of international trade.) But there are disadvantages which argue very strongly against the use of these means, and because of the sentiment among the nations in favor of stable exchange rates it is likely that international trade problems will have to be solved by other approaches.

The approach proposed here relies upon tariffs and subsidies; but it uses these measures in such manner that they give the same general effect as flexible currencies. On the other hand the proposed measures do not have the disadvantages of these latter means. (It is because of the similarity between the proposed scheme and flexible currencies that the application of the proposed means would fall in line with the present operations of the IMF.) While this proposal comes at a time when sentiment among the nations favors the gradual elimination of tariffs and subsidies, it is believed that any apparent retrogression associated with it is illusory, and that in the long run it would be an aid in the removal of trade barriers and inducements.

The proposed innovation, together with its relationship to the whole scheme of control over international trade, may be stated in these terms:

*

1. Each nation will be assigned a figure which will be referred to as its tariff-subsidy rate. As an example, the tariff-subsidy rate of a given nation at a particular time might be 5 percent. Each and every type of goods imported into the given nation will be charged with a tariff at the tariff-subsidy rate, on an ad valorem basis, this tariff being applied in addition to any tariffs that exist independently of the tariff-subsidy rate. This additional tariff is paid by the importer to the given nation in the currency of the given nation. Similarly, each and every type of goods exported from the given nation is favored with a subsidy at the tariff-subsidy rate, in addition to any subsidies that exist inde-

pendently of it. The subsidy is paid by the given nation to the exporter in the currency of the given nation.

The tariff-subsidy rates of the nations are set by an international commission, and are adjusted from time to time. As indicated earlier, the IMF, with modified powers, might serve as the regulating body.

The object of the international commission in adjusting the tariff-subsidy rates of the several nations will be to keep the balances of payments neutral in all nations.

*

2. The tariffs and subsidies applied through the tariff-subsidy arrangement must be considered non-discriminatory by virtue of their uniformity. When the tariff-subsidy arrangement is introduced into any nation, it will have no direct bearing on the existing schedule of discriminatory tariffs and subsidies of that nation. With the tariff-subsidy arrangement in force, each nation will continue to employ discriminatory tariffs and subsidies, and the methods of arriving at these barriers and inducements will be the same as they have been in the past. That is, the nations will rely to a large extent on international agreements, but will reserve the right to operate unilaterally in certain areas. With the tariff-subsidy agreement operating to preserve a neutral balance of payments in each nation, the purpose of the discriminatory tariffs and subsidies will be: (a) to protect sectors of the economy which are threatened by foreign competition and which cannot readily adapt to other types of production, and (b) to protect industries which the economy wishes to preserve, or expand, for reasons such as improving national security and making more efficient use of natural resources.

*

3. The nations will have to cooperate, for their mutual benefit, in regulating foreign investments, through known means, such as taxes, subsidies, and positive restrictions. It is not necessarily desirable that the flow of investment funds to and from any nation be in balance. Given an orderly net flow of investment funds to or from a given nation, this can ordinarily be compensated for

through adjustment of the tariff-subsidy rate. However, erratic surges to or from a nation, especially in connection with short-term investment funds, can be troublesome both with regard to maintaining a neutral balance of payments and with regard to internal stability. It is possible that in time, with all economies controlled and with international trade stabilized through mature international policies, there will be litttle tendency for surges in the flow of investment funds to occur. But so long as there are tendencies for surges of this kind to develop, it will be to the mutual advantage of the nations to cooperate in measures that will hold these surges within reasonable bounds.

*

4. Given that a nation has a surplus in the balance of payments, and that its tariff-subsidy rate is zero, correction of the situation will require that the given nation's tariff-subsidy rate be made negative. Under a negative tariff-subsidy rate, exports will be charged with an export duty, and imports will be favored with a subsidy. As an alternative the whole schedule of tariff-subsidy rates of the other nations could be moved upward. (As is discussed in Secton 41, there is no material difference between the two courses, although on the surface there may appear to be a very serious difference.)

*

Study will show that by manipulation of the tariff-subsidy rates the international trade commission can keep the balances of payments neutral in all nations over the long period. Even if a nation manipulates its discriminatory barriers and inducements in a contrary way, this can be overcome by proper regulation of its tariff-subsidy rate. But then it does not appear that any nation will have anything to gain by trying to defeat the objectives of the tariff-subsidy rate.

The nations can use discriminatory barriers and inducements in working out their problems in the same way as they have up to the present. The effect of the tariff-subsidy arrangement will be to simplify the international negotiations on the discriminatory measures, by removing from these negotiations the consideration of bringing about neutral balances of payments. With the balances of payments taken care of by other means, the nations will have a freer hand in working out trade agreements that will be more advantageous and equitable for all parties. The primary objectives of these negotiations, as has been indicated, will be the protection of special sectors of the several economies, or, more generally, improvement of the alignments of the demand in the several economies, as discussed in the following section.

The merits of the tariff-subsidy arrangement may be stated through a comparison of this device with the device of flexible currency exchange rates: (a) Given that a nation has a deficit in the balance of payments, a devaluation of its currency will correct the situation in a manner that does not discriminate against, or in favor of, any type of goods. An increase in the tariff-subsidy rate will have the same effect, and will be felt in the same way by exporters and importers as would the devaluation. (b) Given that a nation has a deficit in the balance of payments, a devaluation of the currency will operate to increase exports and to decrease imports simultaneously. An increase in the tariff-subsidy rate will have the same effect. In contrast, the application of additional tariffs alone would correct the situation, but this would choke off imports, and could seriously deprive the given nation of much-needed goods from abroad. Similarly, subsidies alone could correct the situation, but in the general case the burden on the taxpayers in supplying the funds for the subsidies could be prohibitive. (c) The great disadvantages connected with adjustments of the currency exchange rates, namely disruptive speculative movements and general instability in short-term investment funds, are avoided with the tariff-subsidy arrangement.

If the nations wish to work toward the gradual elimination of all trade barriers and inducements, they should be aided in this endeavor by the tariff-subsidy arrangement. As discriminatory barriers and inducements are removed, any disturbance of the balance of payments in any nation will be compensated for through adjustment of the tariff-subsidy rate. Gradual elimination of the tariff-subsidy rates will require that the nations make continual adjustments in their respective domestic organizations such as will lead to reductions in the tariff-subsidy rates. As an example of how adjustments in the domestic organizations might lead to elimination of the tariff-subsidy rates, it may be said that inflations in certain nations and deflations in other nations could lead to this effect. However, domestic well-being should take precedence over the objective of removing the tariff-subsidy rates, and this objective should be pursued only to the extent that progress can be made without undue sacrifice at home. That is, there should be no distressing inflations or deflations for this purpose. On the other hand, if it is possible to make progress in the elimination of all trade barriers and inducements without undue sacrifice at home, the progress should be more orderly under the tariff-subsidy arrangement than under the existing arrangements in world trade.

It is a common belief that a nation's prosperity tends to increase as the volume of its foreign trade increases, and that therefore each nation should exert itself to the utmost in increasing its foreign trade. It is suggested here that this is a misleading view, that emphasis should be on the quality of foreign trade rather than on the quantity. The nations of the world can profit by international agreements which bring about a favorable distribution of foreign trade, and in general there will be some optimum volume of foreign trade for each nation, but after the optimum volume of foreign trade has been reached, further expansion of trade will have little effect on the prosperity of the nation. (It may, however, be desirable for the sake of closer political ties among the nations.) When this is realized, the nations will be less inclined to concentrate on frantic efforts at capturing larger and larger portions of the foreign markets, and will be more inclined toward working out a beneficial sharing of the markets.

SECTION 14

Distribution of World Trade

The previous section was primarily concerned with the view of the individual nation toward world trade in providing for its own welfare. This, of course, must involve consideration for the welfare of the other nations as well. Here the discussions duplicate those of the previous section to some extent, but amplify on the larger perspective of global negotiations for improving the distribution of world trade.

The discriminatory trade barriers and inducements can be powerful means for bringing about a distribution of world trade that will be beneficial to all nations. International negotiations should aim at using these in a way that will tend to improve the alignment of the demand in each of the nations with respect to its supply capabilities. This can be of especially great importance to some of the smaller nations.

The manner in which the distribution of world trade should be adjusted will become clearer as the nations—particularly the larger ones—move in the direction of full control, of the type proposed here, and clarify their domestic positions. As they do this, the perspective will become clearer as to how adjustments of foreign trade can operate for their common benefit in improving the individual alignments of demand.

In any of the larger nations, such as the United States, natural forces, together with government assistance, should be highly effective in continuously adjusting the supply capabilities to the distribution of demand. But where stubborn problems exist—where heavy regional unemployment will exist unless foreign markets can be found for the goods produced in the sectors involved, or unless foreign competition is suppressed—international trade agreements can be helpful in relieving these difficulties. The smaller, less diversified nations will, of course, be more dependent on this kind of aid than the larger nations.

Some minimum volume of trade will be required in bringing about a reasonably satisfactory state of affairs for all nations. But after this state has been reached, further expansion of world trade can have little significance in promoting a higher degree of prosperity in the nations. If the businessmen of the various nations are sufficiently enterprising to push the volume of trade to a higher level, they should ordinarily be free to do so without either help or hindrance from the governments. But where these efforts tend to interfere with a suitable distribution of world trade, corrective measures must be taken through adjustment of the trade barriers and inducements.

The notion that prosperity continues to rise to higher and higher levels as the volume of foreign trade increases is a false one, and if the governments allow this notion to obscure the outlook, they may be led astray from the more constructive view that emphasis must be on the most favorable distribution of trade. After a reasonably satisfactory arrangement with regard to both volume and distribution has been reached, the returns from pushing volume to higher levels diminish very rapidly.

Under the present arrangements the problem of bringing about the most suitable world trade conditions is complicated by two factors which may readily be dissociated from this problem. First, the nations do not have adequate internal control and rely upon foreign trade to compensate for internal deficiencies. For example, in the United States many lagging sectors of the economy could be brought to a satisfactory status through better internal control of the aggregate demand; yet some of these sectors look for increased foreign markets as a solution for their difficulties. This factor can be dissociated from the problem of world trade distribution through better internal control. Only after a nation has done all it can to improve conditions in the lagging sectors through internal control should it look to foreign trade arrangements for relief in this matter. Otherwise it complicates matters unnecessarily.

Secondly there is the problem of maintaining satisfactory balances of payments. At the present time the nations rely largely on discriminatory barriers and inducements in handling this problem. And in doing so they produce stresses which interfere with the most constructive distribution of trade. This difficulty can be removed through adoption of the proposed tariff-subsidy arrangement. Because of their non-discriminatory nature, adjustments of the tariff-subsidy rates will have a relatively small effect on the distribution of world trade, while having a powerful effect in correcting unsatisfactory balances of payments. This means that in manipulating the discriminatory barriers and inducements, the nations can concentrate on the most desirable distribution of trade and leave the matter of satisfactory balances to adjustment of the tariff-subsidy rates.

If all trade barriers and inducements are to be eliminated in the long run, as appears to be the hope of some economists, the nations must work to eliminate the conditions that make such instruments expedient. This, reasonably, must be a gradual and long-term process. But while this process is going on, trade barriers and inducements, properly used, will be a constructive influence, not to be regarded as an evil any more than internal control should be regarded as an evil. Moreover, it is not clear that the complete elimination of trade barriers and inducements should be a goal of any great importance. Developments will indicate the kind of adjustments the economies must make in reducing the complexities of trade barriers and inducements, and it is likely that the goal of completely removing these devices will assume a position of minor importance where significant internal sacrifices are required of the nations in working toward its achievement.

SECTION 15

Functions of the IMF or Similar Institution

It has been suggested that the IMF might be commissioned to administer the proposed tariff-subsidy system. However, it will still be important for the IMF, or some similarly constituted body, to operate as an international credit agency, after the fashion in which the IMF now operates. The purpose of international credit arrangements will be to minimize the need for adjustments of the tariff-subsidy rates.

In examining the role of international credit, we must consider this proposition: Assuming that the proposed tariff-subsidy scheme has been adopted, there must be some criteria for deciding when an adjustment is to be made in the tariff-subsidy rate of any nation. One such criterion, perhaps the only one that need be considered, will be the reserves of that nation in the form of gold and in the form of credit, such as the IMF can arrange for. Conceivably the nations might, by common agreement, set up a schedule under which each nation would be required to maintain a minimum of such reserves (total of gold and credit), with the understanding that when a nation's reserves have fallen to the prescribed minimum, its tariff-subsidy rate must be adjusted. This means that if a nation's reserves are approaching the prescribed minimum level, and if that nation wishes to forestall an adjustment in its tariff-subsidy rate, it must secure additional credit from the IMF, or its equivalent.

The primary function, then, of the agency in question will be to supply credit for the purpose of reducing the frequency of adjustments in the tariff-subsidy rates of the several nations. In essence, the agency will serve to eliminate the need for adjustment of the tariff-subsidy rate where a nation's international monetary reserves are falling to the critical level, and where it is expected that the adverse flow of money from that nation will continue for only a short term.

But, on the other hand, it must be recognized that where it is expected that an adverse flow of money from a given nation will continue over the long period, the IMF, or equivalent, will be of little use in correcting this condition. A condition of this kind must be corrected through an adjustment of the tariff-subsidy rate.

It may also be noted that the agency in question can be of great importance in supplying credit to a nation faced with a sudden drain of short-term investment funds. This will be true whether or not a change of the tariff-subsidy rate is contemplated for the given nation.

It is clear that as the volume of international trade grows the collective volume of international payment reserves among the nations—gold and international credit—must grow, just as in a business organization the volume of cash reserves must grow with increase in business volume. If the world monetary gold stock does not grow rapidly enough, it must be supplemented by a rising volume of international credit, and the nations must cooperate in providing this credit through an agency such as the IMF.

SECTION 16

Means of Control

In regulating the aggregate demand the government will be guided by the relationship between the actual rate of aggregate demand and the ratc indicated by the projected curve. When the demand rises above or falls below the desired curve, the government will apply corrective measures; the policy as to how far the demand should be allowed to depart from the desired curve before corrective action is taken is discussed in Chapter VIII. The devices the government may employ in regulating the aggregate demand are outlined here.

Control Subsidies

A powerful means by which the government can bring about an upward correction of the demand is that which will be referred to as the device of *control subsidies.* (The term control subsidies is used to distinguish this device from the more general kinds of subsidies, such as those involved in the farm program.) Control subsidies will be virtually synonymous with deficit financing.

The simplest type of control subsidy is a grant of money to the people with funds raised through the sale of government bonds to the banks. A convenient form of control subsidy, however, is a reduction in income taxes, where the reduction in tax receipts is compensated for through deficit financing. In the model economies studied, control subsidies will generally be in the form of direct grants, since there will be no income taxes. For the actual economy contemplated in this hypothesis, control subsidies will be in the form of tax reductions unless otherwise indicated.

It has been recomended by the Commission on Money and Credit that the tax rate on the first income bracket shall be made flexible, subject to adjustment by the executive department, for the sake of controlling the aggregate demand. It is assumed that the controlled economy under consideration has adopted this recommendation with these specific provisions:

*

1. The tax schedule is set up so that when the tax on the first income bracket is at the normal value, there will be a small rate of budgetary surplus. This will be referred to as the *normal budgetary surplus.* The amount of the surplus is discussed in Section 18.

*

2. When an upward correction of the aggregate demand is required, the executive department is empowered to reduce the tax rate on the first income bracket to any extent necessary, no matter how great the required reduction may be. When the tax is below the normal value, the amount of tax receipts lost to the government by virtue of this fact is the amount of the control subsidies.

*

3. When the flexible tax is reduced, the reduction will be continued for at least 3 months in order that the people may plan to spend the tax remissions constructively, as in installment purchases.

*

4. It is assumed that government spending adheres very closely to the budget. This means that as the flexible tax is reduced the rate of budgetary surplus declines and gives way to a deficit. Thus for any sizable rate of control subsidies there will be a comparable amount of deficit financing, so long as the normal budgetary surplus is small.

*

5. As a simplification it will be taken that the amount of government bonds held by all individuals other than banks remains constant. (The effects of changes in this volume are considered in Section 43.) It will also be taken that the government's cash account remains essentially constant. Then when there is a given rate of budgetary surplus, this is also the rate at which the government redeems its bonds from the banks. When there is a budgetary deficit, this is the rate of increase of government bonds held by the banks.

*

6. For convenience the rate of increase in the total amount of government bonds held by the banks will be designated by the symbol Eg.

Restriction of Ep

For convenience the symbol Ep will be used to represent the rate of bank credit expansion, for the economy as a whole, due to private loans and investments. This excludes the component of bank credit expansion due to government borrowing. The terms and concepts relating to the regulation of Ep as a control measure are as follows:

*

7. Restriction of Ep will be the principal means by which the government will prevent excesses of aggregate demand.

*

8. Restriction of Ep will be accomplished through means that are more positive-acting than familiar central bank practice. It is assumed that each bank will be restricted to a quota of

bank credit expansion, based on its resources (deposits plus capital). This is discussed at greater length in Section 43.

*

9. It is a part of the general concept that Ep will always be restricted to some appropriate value. It is not to be thought that Ep will be restricted only when a downward correction of the aggregate demand is required. As is developed in the later discussions, it is held likely that the demand for Ep will generally equal or tend to exceed the value to which Ep is restricted. There may, however, be times at which the demand for Ep will be less than the restricted value, and in such cases the restriction will have little significance.

*

10. It is assumed that the government will never require the banks to contract private credit. That is, Ep may be restricted to zero, but it may not be restricted to a negative value.

Special Measures

As is developed in the later discussions, it appears likely that the device of control subsidies will be sufficiently powerful to deal with any situation in which an upward correction of the aggregate demand is required. If this device were not sufficiently powerful — with the flexible tax reduced to zero — it would be possible to supplement it with additional direct grants.

At times reference will be made to subsidies on investment, such as accelerated tax write-offs. However there is little emphasis on such devices as means of regulating the aggregate demand. It is held that control subsidies, through flexible taxes, will be effective in dealing with all situations, including those in which there is an investment lag. Where subsidies on investment are expedient they will be in the nature of a refinement on the control scheme, not an indispensable part of it.

It is also held likely that restriction of Ep will be adequate for dealing with all tendencies toward excessive aggregate demand. Only in circumstances that may be regarded as revolutionary might this device be inadequate. In such circumstances negative subsidies — such as sales taxes — should be effective in maintaining control. Taxes of this kind should be regarded as emergency measures and should be treated by the legislature as such.

It is possible that in some cases troublesome excesses of demand will appear in certain sectors of the economy even though the aggregate demand is not generally excessive. Here, too, special sales taxes, either as emergency measures or special standby measures, should be effective in preserving orderly markets and suppressing tendencies toward inflation in the affected areas.

SECTION 17

General Notes on Means of Control

The notes presented at this point are enlarged upon in subsequent discussions. It is believed that the brief statements at this point may be helpful as preparation for the later analyses.

*

1. The control subsidies derive their great potential, in effecting upward corrections of the demand, from the deficit financing that attends them when they are used in sizable quantities. By virtue of the deficit financing the government can always drive the aggregate demand to any desired level with a degree of rapidity that will satisfy any reasonable objective. The reason for this is that the deficit financing provides an additional component of demand, of any desired magnitude, without detracting elsewhere from the demand. In contrast, as is discussed in Section 36, it is held that government spending with funds raised through taxation is relatively ineffective as a pump-priming measure; for while the spending adds a component to the aggre-

gate demand, the taxes detract a comparable amount from private expenditures, making for little net gain.

*

2. Since the controlled economy guarantees to keep the aggregate demand at a near-capacity level at all times, no matter how rapidly capacity may advance — the government standing ready to use deficit financing in any amounts necessary — it is probable that the economy will be able to maintain a balanced budget over the long period. (It is also probable that the economy will be able to maintain a moderate budgetary surplus over the long period, in the interest of accelerated growth as discussed in Section 12, if it so chooses.) The theory is that a net budgetary deficit over the long period will occur only if there is a lag in investment. But because of the guarantee of a satisfactory level of aggregate demand at all times, it is likely that investment will be so brisk that net deficit financing will not be needed.

*

3. If the theory stated in item 2 should prove to be incorrect — that is, if there should be a need for net deficit financing over the long period — this should not be cause for concern. So long as the deficit financing is required in keeping the aggregate demand on the desired curve, it will not in any way contribute to the forces of inflation, and will not contribute toward any future instabilities. This is to say that so long as the aggregate demand is kept on the desired curve, the forces of inflation will be the same whether there is a budgetary deficit or a balanced budget, or even a budgetary surplus.

*

4. If the theory stated in item 2 is correct, it may also be possible for the controlled economy to avoid deficit financing in the shorter periods as well as in the long period. If the economy were to operate in this way, control subsidies would never be used in an active capacity; rather they would serve only in a standby capacity as a means for backing up the guarantee of a satisfactory level of aggregate demand. However, it is a part of the hypothesis that smoother control may be effected by rely-

ing upon budgetary deficits and surpluses in the shorter periods, rather than keeping the budget balanced at all times. The specific policies in this matter are as discussed in the following section.

*

5. An implication of item 2, discussed in subsequent sections, particularly Section 28, is that the demand for Ep will generally be so brisk as to keep this quantity at the restricted value.

*

6. The quantitative effects of control subsidies and changes in the value of Ep, in regulating the aggregate demand, are developed in subsequent discussions.

SECTION 18

Policy in Applying the Control Devices

The policy matters treated here deal with the "mix" with which the control measures are applied. For example, if an upward correction of the aggregate demand is required, the executive department has the option of using control subsidies or seeking a higher rate of Ep, through relaxation of restrictions on this quantity. A question, then, is how shall these alternatives be selected or mixed.

The hypothesis offers fairly specific recommendations in this matter. Presented here is a simple outline of these recommendations. The basis for the quantities chosen is discussed in Section 21 and Chapters VI and VIII.

An assumption underlying the policy outlined is that the demand for Ep will always be up to the restricted value of Ep. If this assumption is not valid, the recommendations have little significance, and another policy must be employed, as discussed in Section 38. Another assumption is that at any time the rate of surplus or deficit in the balance of international payments is insignificant. When this is not true, appropriate adjustment should be considered, as discussed in a later section.

The components of the proposed policy are as follows:

*

1. When control is adopted, the normal rate of budgetary surplus, as referred to in Section 16, shall be 0.5 percent of the aggregate demand. For example, if the aggregate demand is 600 billion dollars per year, the budgetary surplus shall be 3 billion dollars per year. It is expected that this surplus, together with the intermittent use of control subsidies, will lead close to a balanced budget over the long period. Refinements to this component of policy may be made on the basis of experience.

The recommendation thus far is based on the assumption that the economy will want a balanced budget over the long period. If it desires a net budgetary surplus over the long period, for the sake of accelerated growth, the normal rate of budgetary surplus must be increased by the amount of the surplus desired. For example, if the economy desires a surplus of 1 percent of aggregate demand over the long period, the normal rate of budgetary surplus must be 1.5 percent of the aggregate demand.

Unless otherwise indicated, it will be assumed that in the controlled economy under consideration the normal rate of budgetary surplus is 0.5 percent of the aggregate demand.

*

2. At all times in which a downward correction of the aggregate demand is *not* required, Ep will be restricted to a value which will be referred to as the *normal rate of Ep,* and which is given by the equation

$$\text{Normal rate of Ep} = s + cZ \qquad \text{(Equation 1)}$$

where: Ep is a percentage of the aggregate demand; s is the normal rate of budgetary surplus, as a percentage of the aggregate demand; Z is the desired rate of rise of the aggregate demand, in percent per year; and c is a coefficient as discussed below.

When control is adopted, c shall be chosen as 0.5. As is discussed in Chapter VI, this should be a suitable value to begin with, but it is likely that experience will indicate the desirability of small adjustments as time goes on.

As has been indicated in item 1, s should be chosen as 0.5 to begin with, assuming that the object is to maintain a balanced budget over the long period. This, too, may be altered on the basis of experience.

Given that *s* and *c* are each 0.5, equation 1 becomes

Normal rate of Ep $= 0.5 + 0.5Z$ (Equation 2)

This is the value that shall be adopted for the normal rate of Ep when control is adopted, assuming that the objective is to maintain a balanced budget over the long period.

*

3. When an upward correction of the aggregate demand is required (at such times Ep will be restricted to the normal rate), control subsidies will applied in any amounts required. The matters of when action shall be taken and how much the rate of control subsidies shall be are matters that will be left to the discretion of the executive. But guides to these matters are discussed at later points, especially in Chapter VIII.

*

4. When a downward correction of the aggregate demand is required, this will be accomplished through reduction of Ep to a value below the normal rate, as given in equation 2. At such times the tax on the first income bracket will be at the normal value, providing for the normal rate of budgetary surplus. Ep will be reduced to any extent necessary in accordance with executive discretion. Guides as to when action shall be taken and what the magnitude of change shall be are indicated in later discussions.

SECTION 19

MUNEY, MUNEY-SAVINGS, NEW-MUNEY-RATE (DEFINITIONS)

In formal economic parlance money applies to all currency in circulation outside of the banks and all bank deposits in the form of checking accounts, or demand deposits. And in formal economic parlance, bank deposits in the form of savings or time accounts are referred to as near-money. In this hypothesis the term *muney* (a standard simplified spelling of money) will refer to all currency in circulation outside of the banks and all bank deposits. The total muney of the economy is the sum of (a) all currency in circulation outside of the banks, and (b) all bank deposits, whether they be time or demand deposits.

In many discussions the distinction between money and muney will not be important. But since muney covers a less restricted field, this term will be used wherever the choice is optional.

Somewhat arbitrarily the total muney of the United States will be taken as the value listed in *Historical Statistics of the United States: Colonial Times to 1957* under *Series X 266.* This quantity is the same as that given in the reports of the Federal Reserve Board as *deposits adjusted and currency outside banks.*

The rate at which the total muney of the economy increases will be referred to as the *new-muney-rate.*

The term *muney-savings* will refer to savings which occur in the form of muney. (Muney-savings do not include savings in the form of government bonds or in any other form which is not muney, as defined here, but which is sometimes thought of as muney.) For any individual the increase in his muney holdings in a given period is his muney-savings in that period. For the economy as a whole, the muney-savings in any period is the summation of the muney-savings of all individuals in that period, and this must be equal to the increase in the total muney of the economy in the given period. Thus, for the economy as a whole the rate of muney-savings is equal to the new-muney-rate. (In common usage accumulations of muney are sometimes referred to as savings. It should be noted, however, that the term muney-savings applies only to *increments* in muney accumlations over some period in question. Muney accumulations will be referred to as such or as muney holdings; they will never be referred to as savings.)

The principal source of new muney is bank credit expansion. A fair approximation to the new-muney-rate is given by the equation

$$\text{new-muney-rate} = \text{Ep} + \text{Eg} + b$$

where *b* is the rate of surplus in the balance of international payments, and Eg, as indicated earlier, is the rate at which the volume of government bonds held by the banks rises.

When the balance of payments may be neglected, we then have the approximation

$$\text{new-muney-rate} = \text{Ep} + \text{Eg}$$

By the assumptions in item 5 of Section 16, Eg is equal to the rate of budgetary deficit. Under these assumptions, with the balance of payments a negligible factor, we have the approximation

$$\text{new-muney-rate} = \text{Ep} + \text{budgetary deficit}$$

or

$$\text{new-muney-rate} = \text{Ep} - \text{budgetary surplus}$$

SECTION 20

Muney and Control

The most direct way of observing how the control devices operate is through the use of models, as is done in Chapter IV. Stated here are certain conclusions which studies of this kind lead to. These relate to the influence of the new-muney-rate in the control scheme.

It may be noted that the control devices outlined in Section 16 have a direct bearing on the new-muney-rate. When control subsidies are employed, these make the new-muney-rate greater than it would otherwise be by the amount of the control subsidies. This follows from the equations of Section 19 and the influence of the control subsidies on the budgetary status. And a change in Ep, through tightening or relaxing the restrictions on this quantity, makes for an equal change in the new-muney-rate.

It is a principle of the hypothesis offered that a particular new-muney-rate is required in the controlled economy at any time for keeping the aggregate demand on the desired curve. If the actual new-muney-rate is too high or too low, the aggregate demand will rise above or fall below the desired curve. Correction then requires that the new-muney-rate be adjusted by means of the controls.

It is a concept of this hypothesis that in the controlled economy the people provide a demand for new muney issue in the same way that they provide a demand for any type of goods or services. This demand is represented by a quantity which will be referred to as the (PSM + d), the significance of which is enlarged upon in subsequent discussions. A salient feature of the (PSM + d) is that it is determined by what may be summed up as the decisions of the people concerning investment and saving.

In the controlled economy the government keeps the new-muney-rate at, or near, the demand for new muney, or the (PSM + d), through manipulation of the controls. In general the government does not know precisely what the magnitude of the (PSM + d) is; but by operating the controls so as to keep the aggregate demand close to the desired curve, it keeps the new-muney-rate close to the value of the (PSM + d).

In the non-controlled economy there is a quantity equivalent to the (PSM + d). This is simply the new-muney-rate required to keep the aggregate demand at a reasonably satisfactory level, as determined by the decisions of the people relating to savings and investment. But in the non-controlled economy the new-muney-rate is not geared to correspond with this required rate. For example, when the economy is operating on a balanced budget, the new-muney-rate is roughly equal to Ep, and this is determined only by the decisions directly relating to bank credit expansion in private operations; it is independent of the complex of decisions on investment and saving which determine the new-muney-rate required for a satisfactory state. This dissociation between the actual new-muney-rate and a rate that will satisfy the decisions on saving and investing is held to be responsible for the depressions and booms of the non-controlled economy.

In the United States in certain times, as in the periods 1900-1913, 1923-1929, and 1953 to the present, the ratio of total muney to the annual rate of GNP has shown a strong tendency to remain near 0.5. As is discussed in Chapter VI, it is probable that this tendency will continue if the United States adopts the kind of control recommended in this hypothesis. An implication of this is that over any moderately long period, such as 5 years, the mean new-muney-rate, as a percentage of aggregate demand, will be approximately one-half the mean rate of rise of the aggregate demand, when the latter quantity is expressed in percent per year. For example, if the mean rate of rise of the aggregate demand is 6 percent per year, the new-muney-rate will have a mean value of 3 percent of the aggregate demand. Or, in the long run, for each 1 billion dollars per year that the GNP advances by, the muney of the economy must rise by approximately 0.5 billion dollars.

SECTION 21

NOTES ON CONTROL POLICY

It will be desirable in the controlled economy that Ep be highly stable. The policy stated in Section 18 provides for a fair degree of stability. The depression of Ep for downward corrections of the aggregate demand will be undesirable from the standpoint of prospective borrowers and lenders, but will be a necessary evil. It is possible that some other scheme may be developed to provide for greater stability of Ep than under the proposed scheme, but it must be recognized that the behavior of Ep under the proposed scheme willl be preferable to a continuous variation in an irregular pattern.

In an ideal view, there will be an optimal new-muney-rate at any time, and if the actual new-muney-rate is kept at the optimal value, the aggregate demand will remain on the desired curve. But it will not be possible for the economy to operate in this way. Rather the economy must be content with managing the new-muney-rate so that it oscillates about the optimal curve, with the result that the aggregate demand oscillates about its optimal curve. The policy in Section 18 provides for this type of management.

As has been referred to in the previous section, it is held likely that over any moderately long period—such as 5 years—the average new-muney-rate, as a percentage of aggregate demand, must be close to 0.5 times the average rate of rise of the aggregate demand, in percent per year. The policy in Section 18 has been chosen so as to be consistent with this requirement.

To see how this is so, let it be supposed that the economy desires a balanced budget over the long period. This being so it maintains a normal budgetary surplus at the rate of 0.5 percent of aggregate demand, and equation 2 of Section 18 applies. When neither an upward nor downward correction of the aggregate demand is required, Ep will be as given by equation 2. As an approximation, the new-muney-rate is equal to Ep minus the rate of budgetary surplus. Therefore, according to equation 2, the new-muney-rate will normally be equal to 0.5Z, or half the rate of rise of the aggregate demand. This means that the new-muney-rate will normally be close to the expected long-term mean requirement. When downward corrections of the aggregate demand are required, the new-muney-rate will be below the long-term mean requirement because of the depressed state of Ep. During upward corrections of the aggregate demand, the new-muney-rate will be higher than the long-term mean requirement, because of the control subsidies.

Implicit in equation 2 is the speculation that if the economy maintains a normal budgetary surplus at the rate of 0.5 percent of aggregate demand, this will compensate for the deficit financing required during upward corrections of the aggregate demand and lead close to a balanced budget over the long period. The basis for this speculation is discussed in Chapter VIII.

If the economy desires a budgetary surplus over the long period — say, at a mean value of 1 percent of aggregate demand — it must provide for a normal budgetary surplus at the rate of 1.5 percent of aggregate demand, and then equation 1 applies with c at 0.5 and s at 1.5. Under these values the new-muney-rate is normally close to 0.5 times the rate of rise of the aggregate demand, just the same as when the economy desires a balanced budget over the long period.

It should be noted that an assumption underlying the policy stated is that the surplus or deficit in the balance of payments will be negligible. When this quantity is sizable, it may be expedient for the government to modify the normal rate of Ep in the manner discussed in Section 40.

Another assumption involved is that the volume of government bonds in the hands of individuals other than banks will remain constant (item 5 of Section 16). Modifications to policy for significant changes in this volume are discussed in Section 43.

SECTION 22

Savings, Investment and Control

In a sense this section is a digression. Certain principles of control are presented here in terms of the over-all savings and investment of the economy. These same principles are presented elsewhere, in more precise fashion, in terms of monetary relationships. The reasons for this digression are twofold. First, the discussions at this point may reveal some facets of control that are not revealed in the other discussions. Secondly, since the other discussions deal almost exclusively with monetary relationships, it may appear that they oversimplify by failing to take into account all components of savings and investment. It is one purpose of the observations at this point to indicate how the discussions in terms of monetary concepts do account, implicitly, for all components of savings and investment.

A saving is an increment in wealth over some period, such as any week or any year, in any form whatever. Examples of savings are: an increment in muney holdings, an increment in life insurance equities, the acquisition of additional merchandise inventories, the acquisition of an equity in real estate.

For the economy as a whole, investment in any period refers to the acquisition of new capital assests of a physical nature. These include durable producers' goods, increments to merchandise inventories, and new construction of all kinds.

It is sometimes said that for the economy as a whole the net savings in any period must be equal to the net investment in that period. This, however, is only approximately true and must be qualified. A more comprehensive statement of the relationship between savings and investment for the economy as a whole for any period is given by this equation:

Net private investment by people of given economy in given economy	=	Net savings by people of given economy in assets within the economy	+	Governm't budgetary surplus	+	Deficit in balance of internat'l payments

(Equation 3)

Given that the balance of payments is neutral in the long run, and of secondary importance in any shorter period under consideration, the last term of the above equation vanishes. Then the equation, stated in abbreviated form is:

Private investment	=	Private savings	+	Budgetary surplus

(Equation 4)

or

$$\text{Private investment} = \text{Private savings} - \text{Deficit financing} \qquad \text{(Equation 5)}$$

Proceeding from these equations, the following principles may be stated:

*

1. At certain times it will be necessary or expedient for the controlled economy to operate with a budgetary deficit. At these times the rate of private savings will exceed the rate of private investment, as shown by equation 5. The deficit financing in progress will be required because the economy cannot bring private savings and investment into balance, and at the same time keep the aggregate demand on the desired curve, or because it is not expedient to take measures that will bring the two quantities into balance.

*

2. It is held probable in this hypothesis that the controlled economy can keep savings and investment in balance over the long period through regulation of the interest rate. This is discussed at length elsewhere in terms of monetary relationships. It may also be possible for the economy to maintain balance between the two quantities in the shorter periods, through regulation of the interest rate. But it is held likely that for the sake of effecting smoother control it will be preferable for the government to follow policies which lead to budgetary deficits and surpluses in the shorter periods, as will be true of the policies set forth in Section 18.

*

3. For the sake of accelerating the growth rate, the economy may choose to maintain a budgetary surplus over the long period. This course will be indicated where the government is able to induce a rate of investment that exceeds the rate of savings, and where the people are sufficiently intent upon an accelerated growth rate to be willing to support the budgetary surplus, the taxation being higher in this case than it would be with a balanced budget.

Equation 4 shows that the rate of investment will be higher than the rate of savings by the amount of the budgetary surplus. But as is discussed at length in Section 30, it will not be possible for the government to maintain a budgetary surplus and at the same time keep the aggregate demand on the desired curve unless the tendency toward investment is suitably high in relation to the rate of savings. Means by which the government may induce a higher rate of investment are reduction of the interest rate and special subsidies on investment. The government may also employ special means for inducing a higher rate of savings; but it is where these fail to produce the desired effect that the government should give attention to the course of a budgetary surplus.

*

4. While it is not likely that the controlled economy will have to operate with a budgetary deficit over the long period, it must be recognized that there is a small chance that this kind of operation will be necessary. It is held that in this case there will be no adverse side-effects, and that the deficit financing will be inescapable in order to accommodate the free choice of the people with regard to their decisions on investing and saving. One disadvantage of the deficit financing, as revealed by equation 5, is that the growth rate will be lower than it would be if the deficit financing could be eliminated through inducement to a higher rate of investing. When deficit financing is necessary over the long period, the government should, and will, do its utmost to stimulate a higher rate of investment; but after the government has done all it can along such lines, through measures consistent with free enterprise, any remaining deficiency in investment must be compensated for through a budgetary deficit.

*

5. An important principle of control is stated elsewhere in this hypothesis in terms of monetary relationships; the same principle is stated here in terms of savings and investment. In some ways the terms used here are lacking in precision, and therefore what is said may not be convincing; but it is hoped that the validity of the arguments will become plainer when

these are enlarged upon in monetary terms. The principle in question consists of the following component parts:

a. The relationship between savings and investment is in itself of little importance in determining the behavior of the economy. To illustrate what is meant by this, let it be supposed that in a given economy the budget is always balanced, so that savings and investment are always equal. In this case the economy is free to operate in a satisfactory manner or it may at any time proceed into a depression or a boom. Thus from the relationship between savings and investment alone it is not possible to know how the economy will behave.

b. The factors determining the behavior of the economy, with regard to the aggregate demand, are savings and investment taken together with an entity which will be referred to as the *tendency-to-save.* It is not a simple matter to define this last factor, but the concept attending it may be stated in this way: The tendency-to-save may differ from the actual rate of savings by virtue of the fact that savings are not always responsive to the decisions directly relating to savings. To illustrate, let it be supposed that a businessman is suffering dissavings because of unfavorable business conditions. Also, let it be supposed that he seeks to eliminate the dissavings through economies, such as laying off workers; but as he effects these economies his sales fall off and his dissavings continue undiminished. Here the individual wants to reduce his dissavings and takes measures to do so, but these measures do not have the desired effect. It is the concept that in this case the individual's tendency-to-save exceeds his actual rate of savings (he wants to reduce his dissavings and algebraically this is the same as saying he wants to increase his savings); and in the summation for all individuals of the economy there may, and generally will, be an imbalance of this kind.

A quantitative definition for the tendency-to-save, for the economy as a whole, is implicit in the monetary relationships considered in the later discussions. However, this definition will not be stated. The reason for this is that the hypothesis depends mainly on the monetary concepts, and the purpose at this point is simply to present certain general impressions concerning the influence of the factor in question. But for this purpose—that is, for a somewhat impressionistic treatment—the tendency-to-save will be treated as though it had been assigned a quantitative definition.

c. For the simplest view concerning the effects of the tendency-to-save, let it be supposed that the budget is always balanced and that the balance of international payments is always neutral, so that savings and investment are always equal. In this case it may be said that when investment is equal to the tendency-to-save, the aggregate demand remains constant. But if the tendency-to-save exceeds investment, the aggregate demand falls. (In this case deficit financing would serve to halt the decline of the aggregate demand. After the aggregate demand had been stabilized, savings would exceed investment by the amount of the deficit financing, confirming that prior to the introduction of the deficit financing the tendency-to-save exceeded investment.) Similarly, when investment exceeds the tendency-to-save, the aggregate demand rises.

d. Continuing with the assumption that savings and investment are always equal, certain quantitative observations may be made as an enlargement on part c. Let it be supposed that the tendency-to-save exceeds investment by 2 percent of the aggregate demand, and that this condition continues indefinitely. It is held that in this case aggregate demand will fall steadily at a rate in the region of 6 percent per year. (This is discussed in monetary terms in Section 24.) This fall will continue indefinitely. That is, in the first year the aggregate demand will fall by 6 percent, in the second year it will fall another 6 percent, and so on. It is held that depressions (and booms) generally occur in a similar manner—through a relatively small, but persistent, perversity in the relationship among savings, investment, and the tendency-to-save.

e. For a more general statement concerning the influence of the tendency-to-save, let it be supposed that there is a constant rate of deficit financing, with a neutral balance of international payments, making the rate of savings greater than the rate of investment by the amount of the deficit financing. In this case it may be said that if the tendency-to-save exceeds investment by the actual excess of savings over investment, the aggregate demand will remain constant. If the tendency-to-save exceeds investment by more than the actual excess of savings over investment, the aggregate demand will fall. If the tendency-to-save exceeds investment by less than the actual excess of savings over investment, the aggregate demand will rise.

f. In still more general terms, it may be said that the quantity controlling the behavior of the aggregate demand is the quantity Q, where this is given by the relationship:

$$Q = \left(\text{investment} - \begin{matrix}\text{tendency-}\\ \text{to-save}\end{matrix}\right) - (\text{investment} - \text{savings}) \qquad \text{(Equation 6)}$$

And this may be reduced to the form:

$$Q = \text{savings} - \text{tendency-to-save} \qquad \text{(Equation 7)}$$

When Q is zero, the aggregate demand remains constant. When Q is positive, the aggregate demand rises. When Q is negative, the aggregate demand falls. Also, the quantitative behavior is the same as in item d. For example, if Q is 2 percent of the aggregate demand, the aggregate demand rises at a rate in the region of 6 percent per year.

At an earlier point it was said that the behavior of the aggregate demand is a function of savings, investment, and the tendency-to-save. On the other hand, equation 7 indicates that the behavior of the aggregate demand may be regarded as a function of just savings and the tendency-to-save. It may therefore seem improper to refer to investment as one of the factors influencing the aggregate demand. But this view is not justified. To illustrate, let it be supposed that at some time savings and investment are equal. Then the behavior of the aggregate demand is as much a function of investment as it is of savings.

g. In the controlled economy Q must always be of the proper magnitude to keep the aggregate demand rising at the desired rate. One way of adjusting Q is through a budgetary deficit (or surplus). The effect of a budgetary deficit is best seen in connection with equation 7. As the deficit rises, the rate of savings rises, because of the increase in muney-savings. This raises Q and makes for an upward correction of the aggregate demand. (Changes a fall to a rise or increases the rate of rise.)

h. Another way of adjusting Q is through a reduction (or increase) in Ep. This, too, operates by changing the rate of savings in changing the rate of muney-savings. When Ep is reduced, the rate of savings and Q fall, bringing about a downward correction of the aggregate demand.

i. An important means through which Q is regulated in the controlled economy is regulation of the interest rate. To illustrate, let it be supposed that over some period the economy avoids a budgetary surplus or deficit, with the balance of international payments neutral. Then, over this period Q is equal to the quantity (investment — tendency-to-save). Lowering the interest rate increases investment, and to some extent it decreases the tendency-to-save. This increases Q. Raising the interest rate has the opposite effect. It is held that the interest rate will serve as a powerful means by which Q can be kept at the proper value while maintaining a balanced budget over the long period.

This view is consistent with the view in classical theory relating to the function of the interest rate in the non-controlled economy. However, as is discussed at greater length in Section 28, it is held that the interest rate will have a much more systematic and powerful influence in the controlled economy than in the non-controlled economy because of the guarantee of a continuously prosperous state.

*

In Section 20 it was argued that the aggregate demand can be held on the desired course only by keeping the new-muney-rate at a value equal to the quantity referred to as the (PSM + d). Moreover, it was held that this is the only condition necessary for keeping the aggregate demand on the desired curve. It may seem that this view fails to give weight to all the non-monetary factors entering into savings and investment, and that it may be inconsistent with the views stated above regarding the interaction of fiscal and monetary policies with savings and investment. It is submitted, however, that this is not so. As has been stated in Section 20, and as will be enlarged upon from time to time, the (PSM + d) is determined by the decisions of the people relating to all forms of savings and investment. Implicit in this is that when the new-muney-rate is equal to the (PSM + d), fiscal and monetary policies are such that they serve to keep Q in equation 6 at the proper value.

For the most part the hypothesis makes little direct reference to the component principles under item 5. It is more convenient to talk in monetary terms. But the discussions in monetary terms will always be consistent with these principles, and will, in effect, amplifiy on them.

In anticipation of the later discussions, the correlation between the monetary concepts and the concepts in terms of over-all savings and investment may be stated more concretely in this way: The new-muney-rate, which is also the rate of muney-savings, is one component of over-all savings. At any time there is a particular new-muney-rate which will bring the over-all rate of savings into balance with the tendency-to-save, and thus cause the aggregate demand to remain constant. This new-muney-rate is what is referred to as the PSM (defined presently in terms of monetary concepts). But in the controlled economy it will ordinarily be required that the aggregate demand rise at some steady pace. Therefore it will be necessary that over-all savings exceed the tendency-to-save by some appropriate margin. The new-muney-rate required to bring about this relationship is what is referred to as the (PSM + d).

SECTION 23

The PSM, the (PSM + d)

The PSM is a symbol representing a quantity which will be referred to as the *propensity-to-save-muney.* (The hyphenated spelling is used to distinguish this term from the term *propensity to save money* which has been used for other purposes.) This quantity is of interest for the non-controlled economy as well as the controlled economy, and may be defined, subject to certain qualifications, in this way: Let it be supposed that in the non-controlled economy the aggregate demand has been falling steadily. Also, let it be supposed that the government contemplates intervening to stabilize the aggregate demand (causing it to level off at some constant value) through the use of control subsidies. If the government should intervene in this way, its action will cause the new-muney-rate to rise. It is a principle of the hypothesis that in this case there will be a particular value to which the new-muney-rate must be raised, subject to the qualification indicated below. (This principle is illustrated in the model cases in Chapter IV.) This new-muney-rate — required for stabilizing the aggregate demand — is the PSM. Beyond this it may be said that the magnitude of the PSM at any time is determined by the decisions of the people concerning investing and saving. (This too is illustrated in the models in Chapter IV.)

The qualification referred to above is that there is an approximation implicit in this definition of the PSM. This arises from the fact that the new-muney-rate required for stability of the aggregate demand at any time will depend upon the means by which the new-muney-rate is altered. But it is submitted that a similar simplification is present in the Keynesian principle that a particular rate of investment is necessary to sustain a given level of aggregate demand. (That is, Keynes did not consider refinements incident to changes in the distribution of investment.) The Keynesian simplification is of little importance, and the one used here should be of equally small importance.

It follows from the observations to this point that when the aggregate demand is declining, the PSM exceeds the existing new-muney-rate. For then deficit financing would serve to stabilize the aggregate demand, and, all other things remaining unchanged, the new-muney-rate after stabilization would be greater than the existing new-muney-rate by the amount of the deficit financing. Conversely it may be said that when the PSM exceeds the new-muney-rate, the aggregate demand declines. Similarly, when the PSM is less than the new-muney-rate, the aggregate demand rises.

An excess of the new-muney-rate over the PSM has the same significance as Q in equations 6 and 7 of Section 22. A small, persistent perversity in the relationship between the PSM and the new-muney-rate can cause a major depression or boom, and it is held that in general depressions and booms occur in just this way.

The (PSM + d) is a quantity which is of interest in the controlled economy, when it is the object to keep the aggregate demand on a desired curve that is rising continuously, as should always be the case. If it were the object to keep the aggregate demand constant, then it would be necessary for the government to keep the new-muney-rate equal to the PSM. But since it will be the object to keep the aggregate demand on a steadily rising curve, it will be necessary for the government to keep the new-muney-rate greater than the PSM by some differential which is designated as d. Thus the (PSM + d) is the new-muney-rate that is present when the aggregate demand does follow the desired curve.

Whether the PSM be considered by itself or as a component of the (PSM + d) it is always determined by the decisions of the people relating to investing and saving. In the non-controlled economy the PSM is largely a function of the state of mind of the economy—the degree of optimism or pessimism present—and to a lesser extent is a function of the major tangible factors of the economy, such as the level of aggregate demand and the volume of muney. Because of the wide fluctuations in the state of mind in the non-controlled economy, the PSM varies through a wide range and is relatively unstable. In the controlled economy the PSM is relatively stable and varies through a relatively narrow range, because of the stability of the state of mind.

The factor d is a stable quantity, and its magnitude is determined by the rate at which the desired curve of aggregate demand rises, as is discussed in the following section.

SECTION 24

A Quantitative Speculation

The speculation presented at this point is concerned with the quantitative aspects of the relationships in the preceding section. The basis for this speculation is discussed at some length in the book referred to in Chapter I.

It has been observed that when the PSM exceeds (or is less than) the new-muney-rate, the aggregate demand falls (or rises). The speculation submitted is this: First, the rate at which the aggregate demand falls will be roughly proportional to the excess of the PSM over the new-muney-rate. Secondly, given that the PSM exceeds the new-muney-rate by X percent of the aggregate demand, the aggregate demand will fall at a rate in the region of 3X percent of itself per year. The same ratio applies when an excess of the new-muney-rate over the PSM causes the aggregate demand to rise.

More generally, it is estimated that the ratio in question lies somewhere between 2 and 4. But as a simplification it will generally be taken that this ratio is exactly 3. It is believed that the sense of the discussions employing this simplification will not be seriously affected by any inaccuracies entailed.

One implication of this speculation is that a moderate excess of the PSM over the new-muney-rate will cause a major depression within a fairly short period of time. For example, an excess in the amount of 5 percent of the aggregate demand will cause the aggregate demand to decline by close to 30 percent over a period of 2 years. The mechanics involved are illustrated in the models of Chapter IV, and it is held that the processes illustrated are representative of those that occur in any depression experienced by the non-controlled economy.

One application of this speculation is in estimating what the value of d in the (PSM + d) must be. This value must be close to one-third of the yearly percentage rise of the desired curve of aggregate demand. For example, if in a given year the desired aggregate demand rises by 6 percent of itself, then d must be close to 2 percent of the aggregate demand.

In addition the given speculation provides a basis for estimating the PSM in the United States in any past period. In this type of determination the PSM for any period, such as any year, is taken as the value given by the equation: Z = 3(S — PSM), where: Z is the percentage rise of the aggregate demand, or GNP, in that period; S is the rise of the total muney, as a percentage of aggregate demand, in that period; and the PSM is the mean value for the given period, as a percentage of the aggregate demand.

Because of such things as lags in the response of the aggregate demand to changes in the other variables, determinations of this kind have certain deficiencies. But it is held that the values obtained in this way provide a useful index for the purposes to which they are applied.

SECTION 25

Comparison With Multiplier Theory

The Keynesian multiplier theory argues that the level of aggregate demand is determined by the rate of investment, and that a given increase in the rate of investment will produce an increase in the aggregate demand equal to several times—such as 2 to 3 times—the increase in the rate of investment. Seemingly as an extension of this theory, it is sometimes believed that if a given rate of deficit financing is introduced into an economy, the aggregate demand will rise by an amount in the order of 2 to 3 times the given rate of deficit financing.

This belief may appear to be of essentially the same substance as the views stated in the preceding section. It is submitted, however, that any apparent similarity is misleading.

To illustrate, let it be supposed that in a non-controlled economy the PSM remains constant over some period at the value of 2 percent of the aggregate demand, no matter how the aggregate demand may vary, and that in the same way Ep remains constant at 2 percent of the aggregate demand. Also, let it be supposed that to begin with the budget is balanced, and that the balance of international payments is neutral. Then the PSM is equal to the new-muney-rate, and the aggregate demand remains constant. But now, let is be supposed that the government wishes to bring about a rise in the aggregate demand, and that it proceeds to employ deficit financing at the rate of 3 percent of the aggregate demand. The question is how will the aggregate demand behave.

It is doubtful that economists have ever encountered this question stated in terms essentially the same as those used here. But it does seem that if this question were translated into the terms that are commonly used, then the answer of many economists, on the basis of multiplier theory, would be that the aggregate demand must rise by an amount in the region of from 6 to 9 percent, and must then remain at that level until some other influences arise to disturb it. It would seem, for example, that such an answer is clearly implied in the views stated by Prof. Alvin H. Hansen in *A Permanent Tax Cut Now, Challenge, October 1962.*

But in the views of this hypothesis this answer is incorrect. According to the principles outlined and speculated upon thus far, the aggregate demand will rise at the rate of approximately 9 percent per year, and will continue to do so so long as the PSM and Ep and the rate of deficit financing remain as assumed. Thus over a period of 3 years the aggregate demand will rise by approximately 30 percent of its value at the beginning of that period, and after that it will still be in the process of rising.

SECTION 26

GENERAL BEHAVIOR CHARACTERISTICS OF THE PSM AND EP

Some general characteristics of the behavor of the PSM and Ep may best be presented by considering them in connection with the non-controlled economy as well as the controlled economy. These characteristics, as amplified upon in later discussions, are as follows:

*

1. In the non-controlled economy the PSM is strongly influenced by the state of mind of the economy — the degree of optimism or pessimism prevalent. As the state of mind becomes increasingly pessimistic (or optimistic) the PSM tends to rise (or fall). More specifically, it may be said that in effect the real variables of the economy — total muney, aggregate demand, etc. — determine certain limits within which the PSM is free to vary; but the position of the PSM within these limits is determined by the state of mind. When the PSM is near the upper limit, this reflects a highly pessimistic state of mind, and when it is near the lower limit, this reflects a highly optimistic outlook.

In another view it may be said that the PSM is strongly influenced by the inclination toward investment. The PSM experiences a component fall (or rise) as the inclination toward investment rises (or falls). Similarly the rate of purchase of durable consumer goods has a strong influence on the PSM.

*

2. In the controlled economy the PSM behaves in the same general manner as in the non-controlled economy. However, because the state of mind will be more stable in the controlled economy, the range of variation of the PSM for any array of the real variables will be much narrower than in the non-controlled economy.

*

3. In the non-controlled economy the value of Ep is strongly influenced by two factors, namely, the state of mind and the interest rate. In general the dominant effect is that produced by the state of mind. This is to say that because of the lack of controlled conditions and the extent to which the state of mind may vary, there is no systematic relationship between the value of Ep and the interest rate. To illustrate, let it be supposed that at some time the interest rate is reduced by a substantial amount. This should lead to an increase in Ep. But it is possible that an adverse change in the state of mind will occur and will cause Ep to decrease despite the reduction in the interest rate.

What has been said for Ep applies to the new-muney-rate as well, since in the non-controlled economy Ep ordinarily constitutes the bulk of the new-muney-rate.

*

4. In the controlled economy there will be a highly systematic and sensitive relationship betwen the interest rate and the demand for Ep, because of the continuously favorable prospects for investment. (Since Ep will generally be restricted to a particular value, it is preferable to speak of the demand for Ep as a function of the interest rate rather than Ep itself.) This demand will rise (or fall) as the interest rate falls (or rises).

*

5. In the controlled economy the PSM may be expected to rise (or fall) as the interest rate rises (or falls). However, it is possible that the magnitude of this effect will be so small as to be of minor importance.

SECTION 27

Over-all Credit Expansion and Ep

The matter of interest at this point is the relationship among these quantities: the interest rate, the rate of bank credit expansion in private operations, Ep, and the over-all expansion of credit in all forms.

A function of the interest rate is to establish equilibrium between the supply and demand for Ep. But it must also establish equilibrium between the supply and demand in the over-all expension of credit in all forms. In this study primary attention will be given to the matter of how the interest rate brings the supply and demand for Ep into balance. It may seem, therefore, that the other forms of credit are being neglected. However, reflection will show that this is not so. For if the supply and demand for Ep are in balance, there must be equilibrium in the over-all supply and demand for credit; any imbalance in the over-all sphere must spill over into the area of bank credit, and only after balance has been achieved in the over-all sphere can there be balance with regard to Ep.

Therefore, in considering how the interest rate establishes equilibrium between the supply and demand for Ep, we are at the same time considering how the interest rate establishes equilibrium in the over-all supply and demand for credit.

SECTION 28

Probable Mode of Behavior of the Controlled Economy

There are many modes of operation which may be anticipated for the controlled economy, although some of these are highly improbable. Outlined here is the mode held to be the most probable, to be referred to as the *probable mode*. The broad features of this mode are: first, that the economy seeks a balanced budget over the long period, second, that Ep is regulated in accordance with the provisions of Section 18, and third, that Ep is always at the restricted level, with possible exceptions of minor importance.

A matter of some interest in connection with this mode is that under it the economy behaves in a manner which bears a strong resemblance to the behavior of the non-controlled economy envisaged in classical theory.

Elements of the manner in which the economy operates when in the probable mode are as follows:

*

1. When a downward correction of the demand is required, the government will reduce Ep to some value below the normal rate. It is to be expected that immediately after this change the demand for Ep will exceed the supply. But it is also to be expected that the interest rate will rise and that this process will continue until the demand for Ep is equal to the supply.

It may be noted that in this case the interest rate has a function similar to that in classical theory. But it must also be noted that there are important distinctions. In classical theory, when Ep is too high, natural forces cause the interest rate to rise, and this causes Ep to fall. In the controlled economy governmental action causes Ep to fall, and the rise in the interest rate is a result of this action.

*

2. When the government seeks to restore Ep to the normal rate, from a depressed level, the matter is very different. Here the government cannot bring about an increase in Ep with the same directness as in effecting a reduction. The government is limited to relaxing the restrictions on Ep and inducing a decrease in the interest rate. The means by which the government can induce a reduction of the interest rate are not a direct form of control, but rather may be looked upon as a form of guidance. This is discussed in Section 43.

Although the government will be able to exert great pressures in effecting reductions of the interest rate, as required, there will, at any time, be some level below which the interest rate cannot be driven by means that are reasonably consistent with free enterprise. This level will be referred to as the *lowest realizable* interest rate, and the region above it will be referred to as the realizable range.

The question that now arises is whether or not the required increase in Ep can always be brought about, through reduction of the interest rate, before the lowest realizable interest rate has been reached. For if Ep is still deficient after the interest rate has reached the lowest possible value, and if conditions of this kind are other than a rarity, the economy cannot operate in the probable mode. Net deficit financing will be required over the long period.

The hypothesis holds it to be highly probable that the answer to this question is in the affirmative. The feature that makes this behavior possible is the guarantee of a satisfactory level of aggregate demand at all times. Under this guarantee the demand for Ep will be highly responsive to changes in the interest rate, and it is held probable that at the lowest realizable interest rate the demand for Ep will always be far greater than the normal rate of Ep as given in equation 2 of Section 18.

In the more optimistic periods in the United States, as in 1955, the demand for Ep has been such as tends to bear out this argument. It is held that under the guarantee of a satisfactory level of aggregate demand the demand for Ep will always be as brisk as it has been in these optimistic periods. A more powerful argument for this view is that presented by Dr. Simon Kuznets in his study *Capital in the American Economy; Its Formation and Financing.*

It is, of course, possible that this theory is incorrect, in which case net deficit financing will be required over the long period. This is one of the less probable modes of behavior, discussed in Section 30.

Again it may be noted that the behavior of the controlled economy in the probable mode is similar to the behavior of the non-controlled economy in classical theory. Classical theory also holds that there will always be an interest rate within the realizable range at which Ep will be sufficiently large to maintain a satisfactory state. But again there are notable distinctions between classical theory and the theory for the controlled economy. The major distinction is that in the controlled economy reduction of the interest rate to the lowest realizable level causes the demand for Ep to be greater than it need ever be because of the optimistic outlook maintained. When the guarantee of a satisfactory level of aggregate demand is removed, as in classical theory—that is, when the economy is free to lapse into a pessimistic state of mind—it is no longer true that reduction of the interest rate to the lowest realizable value must bring the value of Ep to a satisfactory level, or better. This is the principle reason for the failure of classical theory. A second distinction between the two theories is that whereas classical theory relies upon natural forces in effecting needed reductions of the interest rate, the theory of the controlled economy depends in some measure on government intervention.

SECTION 29

A Theory of Depressions and Booms

In the most elementary view, depressions and booms (in the non-controlled economy) occur because there are no forces that will systematically keep the PSM and the new-muney-rate in a satisfactory relationship with each other. Another way of saying this is that there are no forces that will keep the quantities on the right hand side of equations 6 and 7 of Section 22 in a satisfactory relationship. As has been observed, a persistent excess of the PSM over the new-muney-rate will cause a depression, and a persistent imbalance in the other direction may cause an inflationary boom. It is held that there are no forces to prevent imbalances of this kind.

Going a step further, however, it may be perceived that when the economy moves in the direction of a depression or a boom, there is an element of systematic behavior, but in a perverse sense. This is a tendency of the economy to follow a course that clearly resembles psychosomatic illness in humans, and which will be referred to as psychosomatic behavior. In this course psychological causes and the real manifestations induced by them feed on each other and reinforce each other in the familiar vicious cycle.

As has been observed, the PSM and the new-muney-rate are strongly influenced by the state of mind of the economy. In general, as the state of mind becomes increasingly pessimistic, the PSM rises and the new-muney-rate falls. Either effect, by itself, contributes toward an excess of the PSM over the new-muney-rate, and thus toward a downward movement of the aggregate demand; together the effects are additive. Thus in a depression we have this perverse chain: A pessimistic outlook causes the PSM to exceed the new-muney-rate; this causes the aggregate demand to fall; and the decline of the aggregate demand reinforces the pessimistic outlook, completing the closed, vicious loop. A similar chain exists in the course of a boom.

A question that now arises is this: Granting that some depressions are explainable in terms of psychosomatic behavior, is it not possible that depressions are sometimes the result of functional causes, in the same way that some human illnesses are due to functional disorders even though psychosomatic behavior is at first suspected?

In order to examine this matter it is necessary that we have a working concept of what a functional cause of depressions is. It is suggested that a functional cause of depressions may be defined as a condition which would survive if the economy were to adopt control, and which would then make it necessary for the economy to employ deficit financing on a sustained basis in maintaining a satisfactory state, with the interest rate at the lowest realizable level.

It is held likely that there have never been any functional causes of depressions, as just defined, in any modern economy.

Most theories advanced in explaining depressions imply the existence of functional causes, but none has been successful in bringing any clearly to light. For example, one theory holds that there must be a chronic or cyclical lag in investment. But the basis for this theory seems to be only the experience of the noncontrolled economy, which may readily be explained in terms of psychosomatic behavior. The theory does not present any evidence that chronic or cyclical lags in investment must occur under controlled conditions. Similarly, theories relating to overproduction (technocracy, automation), or underconsumption, simply state symptoms of psychosomatic behavior, without exposing any functional causes.

A theory of some interest is one which explains a particular recession in terms of functional causes. This is the theory of the President and his advisers to the effect that the recent lag in activity in the United States has been due to excessively burdensome taxes. This is discussed at length in Section 39 and Chapter III. It is held that this theory is just one more tenuous argument in explaining a situation which may so easily be explained in terms of psychosomatic behavior.

Another theory of interest is that advanced by Keynes. Here the functional cause is diminishing returns to capital. In Keynesian theory, as in most theories, the depression starts with a decline in investment and this is aggravated by subsequent psychosomatic complications. In Keynesian theory the initial decline in investment is attributed to a decline in the return on investment. But it is important to note that in explaining the fall in investment, Keynes is primarily concerned with the *prospective* return rather than with the present return (this is his *marginal efficiency of capital*); and he uses psychological factors in explaining the decline in expectations far more than he does any existing manifestations of a decline in the return. His strongest statement on the influence of the actual decline in return, in *The General Theory of Employment, Interest and Money,* Chapter 22, is this:

> Let us return to what happens at the crisis. So long as the boom was continuing, much of the new investment showed a not unsatisfactory current yield. The disillusionment comes because doubts suddenly arise concerning the reliability of the prospective yield, *perhaps because the current yield shows*

signs of falling off, as the stock of newly produced durable goods steadily increases. (Italics not Keynes'.)

As a digression, notice may be taken of the absurdity in speaking of a disillusionment as resulting from nothing more than doubts. Not only is this association of ideas absurd, but it would seem insidious to imply that there is a situation ripe for disillusionment when all that is meant is that there is a situation susceptible to fears. But more to the point is the italicized portion of this passage. This clearly indicates the extent to which Keynes has been able to establish a link between depressions and the trend of the return on investment. If we should write off the importance of any actual diminution of the return on capital, as so many economists appear to have done — and Keynes' luke-warm convictions do not seem to argue strenuously against this — then it follows that Keynesian theory, for all its abstruseness, is just another way of stating the theory of psychosomatic behavior.

SECTION 30

Less Probable Modes of Operation

Considered here are certain other modes of operation (other than the probable mode, as discussed in Section 28) which may be anticipated for the non-controlled economy. With one exception these modes are undesirable, and it is held unlikely that the economy will be obliged to operate in any of these. The mode referred to as the budgetary surplus mode may be considered desirable for the sake of an accelerated growth rate, but it is somewhat doubtful that there will be a great deal of interest in an accelerated growth rate when it is found that it is just as easy to maintain a satisfactory level of employment with a normal growth rate (as defined in Section 12) as it is with an accelerated growth rate.

Investment Deficiency Mode

In the investment deficiency mode the interest rate is at the lowest realizable value and Ep is not sufficient to keep the aggregate demand on the desired curve, making it necessary for the government to employ deficit financing.

It is a part of the hypothesis that this mode is not likely to occur in the foreseeable future in any economy adopting control. But let it be supposed that this mode does occur; moreover, let it be supposed that this mode continues indefinitely and that the rate of deficit financing required is quite heavy, such as 10 percent of aggregate demand. The question then is whether or not this rate of deficit financing must be an unwholesome element — as held in conservative theory — and must have harmful side-effects.

Through their spending decisions the people demand new muney at a certain rate, the value of the (PSM + d). This demand must be satisfied if the aggregate demand is to remain on the desired curve. But under the assumed conditions the new-muney-rate in the absence of deficit financing — the rate determined mainly by the decisions directly affecting Ep — is not adequate to satisfy this demand for new muney. The remedy, therefore, is in deficit financing to bring the new-muney-rate up to the required level.

The only thing unwholesome in this situation is the conservative notion that the new-muney-rate must be decided by the factors directly affecting Ep, even when this quantity is not sufficient to satisfy the demands of the economy. This notion derives from tradition and cannot be justified on the basis of logic. This prejudice must be put aside, and it must be recognized that when Ep fails to meet the requirements of the economy, the deficiency must be made up through deficit financing.

The need for deficit financing can be reduced if the people can be induced to save less wealth in the form of muney, or if the government can induce a higher rate of investment, leading to a greater demand for Ep. In particular the government should aim at stimulating investment—through such means as subsidies on investment—as this will improve the growth rate. It is only after such attempts have fallen short of the mark that deficit financing on a sustained basis will be necessary.

One effect that is commonly thought of as being inseparably linked with deficit financing is that of inflation. As has been indicated, the hypothesis holds that inflation is a function of how the aggregate demand is managed, together with the moral pressures that may be exerted upon the people for abatement of inflationary practices, and that it is independent of such things as deficit financing, the gold content of the dollar, or the character of the muney of the economy from any point of view.

One means by which the people can be induced to save less wealth in the form of muney is through inducing them to purchase government bonds. That is, instead of selling bonds to the banks to increase the new-muney-rate, the government may instead sell bonds to the general public to decrease the new-muney-rate required. It is held, however, that when deficit financing is required on a sustained basis, it will be preferable for the government to sell its bonds to the banks only. As is discussed in Section 43, there is no advantage in selling the bonds to individuals other than banks, and there may be a disadvantage in that the interest burden is likely to be higher.

A fear sometimes entertained in connection with deficit financing is that it will lead to a build-up of the muney accumulations and that eventually a breaking point will be reached, giving rise to disruptive dissavings from muney accumulations. That is, at some point the people will suddenly turn from accumulating muney at a rapid pace to disposing of accumulations at a rapid pace, thereby creating chaotic market conditions. It is submitted that there is little reason to anticipate an abrupt change of this kind.

A quantity of interest in this connection is the ratio of the total muney of the economy to the annual rate of aggregate demand. This will be represented by the symbol R. If there is a tendency toward a rapid increase in the total muney due to deficit financing, what happens to R will be more significant than the behavior of the muney. The theory here, discussed at length in the book referred to in Chapter I, is that as R rises the (PSM + d), or the new-muney-rate, will decline. This will cause the rate of rise of R to taper off. But all developments of this kind should be gradual. It is true that a build-up of R will lead toward a correction, as held in the alarmist theory referred to above. But the correction should not be an abrupt change from a high rate of muney-savings to a high rate of muney-dissavings. The correction should be a gradual decline in the rate of muney-savings toward some equilibrium condition.

Transient Muney-dissavings Mode

It is held unlikely that the people will ever be disposed toward making such heavy dissavings from muney accumulations as will make the (PSM + d), or the required new-muney-rate, negative. However, it is possible that a condition of this kind will occur under revolutionary circumstances of an unforeseeable nature. But a state of this kind — which may be referred to as the transient muney-dissavings mode — is necessarily an unstable one and must have a limited duration.

To illustrate the behavior of the economy under a state of this kind, we may suppose that the (PSM + d) is minus 1 percent of the aggregate demand, so that the new-muney-rate must be minus 1 percent of aggregate demand. In this case Ep will be restricted to zero, and the flexible tax on the first income bracket will be at the normal value. Assuming that the normal budgetary surplus is 0.5 percent of the aggregate demand, it will be necessary for the government to apply special taxes, such as sales taxes, in the amount of 0.5 percent of the aggregate demand, in order that the new-muney-rate shall be minus 1 percent of aggregate demand.

That this mode is unstable follows from the fact that under it the total muney of the economy diminishes and this cannot continue indefinitely. In the larger view the developments depend on the behavior of R, as referred to above. As R falls the (PSM + d) is corrected, and in time this quantity must move out of the negative region.

When the (PSM + d) is so highly negative as to require special taxes, any form of taxes will have a corrective effect; but the time lags will be greater for some forms of taxes than for others. (The discussions in Chapter VIII indicate, in some measure, the processes involved). With a highly negative (PSM + d) it is likely that fairly strong excesses of demand will apear in particular sectors of the economy, as in the durable consumer goods and producers' goods sectors. The most expeditious way of dealing with these will be through special sales taxes applied wherever the excesses of demand appear.

The possibility that the (PSM + d) will ever be so highly negative as to require the imposition of distressingly high sales taxes is so remote that it hardly merits serious attention. Yet, if a state of this kind did develop these considerations would apply: First, it is almost certain that the more necessary types of goods and services would not be greatly affected by excessive demand, and that therefore no distressing sales taxes would be required on such items. Secondly, where hardship in procuring goods and services did occur, rationing in the absence of sales taxes — as in wartime emergencies — would be the remedy. Thirdly, the higher the absolute magnitude of the (PSM + d), and the higher the sales taxes, the more rapidly must these elements taper off.

The investment deficiency mode and the mode considered here are held to be equally unlikely. And if the investment deficiency mode should develop, and a heavy rate of deficit financing should be required, the notion that this should lead to the transient muney-dissavings mode is held to be far-fetched. But in any case the possibility that deficit financing may lead to the transient muney-dissavings mode should not be regarded as a valid argument against the use of deficit financing when it is required to preserve a satisfactory state; for this mode does not have any fatal implications.

Budgetary Surplus Mode

In this mode the economy operates with a net budgetary surplus over the long period for the sake of maintaining an accelerated growth rate.

Given that the economy is operating with a balanced budget over the long period, let it be supposed that it desires an accelerated growth rate. A primary requisite is that the government must be able to induce an increase in the rate of investment; for the rate of investment is virtually synonymous with the rate of growth. But if the economy wishes to continue with a balanced budget over the long period, then it must also be able to induce an increase in savings, equal to the desired increase in the rate of investment. For reasons which are suggested presently, this may be quite difficult. An alternative will lie in introducing a budgetary surplus over the long period. Some major implications of operating in this latter mode may be summarized in this way:

*

1. If the government is able to induce the desired increase in the rate of investment but is not able to induce an equal increase in the rate of savings, a budgetary surplus will compensate for the deficiency in savings, as indicated by equation 4 of Section 22.

*

2. It is not necessarily true that introducing a budgetary surplus of a given magnitude will bring about an equal increase in the rate of investment. This will be true only if the rate of savings remains unchanged as the budgetary surplus is introduced. In general the gain in investment will be somewhat lower than the budgetary surplus because of a decrease in the rate of savings. Under highly unfavorable conditions the gain in investment may be only a small fraction of the budgetary surplus.

*

3. The government can introduce a budgetary surplus only when the demand for Ep is sufficiently brisk to support it. The new-muney-rate must always be the value necessary to keep the aggregate demand on the desired curve. Roughly speaking, the new-muney-rate at any time is equal to Ep minus the budgetary surplus. Therefore, when the budgetary surplus is introduced, the value of Ep must be greater than it would otherwise be by the amount of the surplus.

*

4. Inducing a sufficiently brisk demand for Ep must be a part of the government's efforts in stimulating the increased growth rate. It may be that the government can induce the required demand for Ep simply by bringing about a reduction of the interest rate. But it may also be necessary for the government to issue subsidies on investment, as through an accelerated tax write-off.

*

5. When the budgetary surplus is introduced, the rise in taxes involved will bring about a component decrease in savings. This, as discussed in item 2, will detract from the effectiveness of the budgetary surplus. However, this effect should be a small fraction of the budgetary surplus. Savings tend to remain a fixed percentage of take-home income (income after taxes). In recent years in the United States net savings have been in the region of 10 percent of total take-home income. Thus when taxes are raised by the amount necessary to provide the desired budgetary surplus, decreasing total take-home income by that amount, savings should diminish by about 10 percent of that amount. (It is generally held that because of the distinction between marginal and average effects, savings will diminish by considerably more than this value. But it is held here that while savings may diminish by a greater value initially, this effect will be transient, and when conditions have settled out the effect will be as stated. The behavior involved is discussed at length in Section 36.)

*

6. When a budgetary surplus is introduced, the increased availability of funds for investment comes about principally through the rise in Ep that must attend the introduction of the budgetary surplus.

*

7. When Ep is increased by the amount of the budgetary surplus, part of this increment will generally be diverted from increased investment to increased consumption. For example, part of the increase in Ep will go to finance increased installment purchases of consumption goods. The government can minimize effects of this kind by special measures aimed at discouraging the financing of consumption through bank loans.

It is of some interest to note how an increase in bank loans for financing consumption fits into equation 4 of Section 22. When a person secures a bank loan to finance consumption, he makes a dissaving; for he incurs a debt without acquiring an offsetting asset that may be regarded as a form of saving. Thus the increase in bank loans for financing consumption makes for a component decrease in the savings term of the equation, and this makes the investment term lower than it would otherwise be for a given budgetary surplus.

*

The above items deal with the behavior of the economy when the course of a budgetary surplus is followed. The following items deal with the behavior of the economy when it adheres to a balanced budget over the long period. These are presented for the sake of comparison. It is assumed that the economy is operating in the probable mode with a normal growth rate, and that the government wishes to bring on an accelerated growth rate without departing from the balanced budget over the long period.

*

8. If the government maintains a balanced budget and simply proceeds to induce an increase in investment through subsidies on investment, it sets in motion a vicious process. Because of the stimulus, there is an increased demand for savings, and this causes the interest rate to rise. But the rise in the interest rate tends to discourage investment, and therefore this rise must be offset by an increase in the subsidies. Assuming for the moment that the rate of savings does not increase, the government can go on increasing the subsidies indefinitely, and this will simply lead to offsetting increases in the interest rate; but there can be no increase in investment.

But there is another side to the matter. As the interest rate rises one effect will be to induce some increase in the rate of savings. The question, then, is how rapidly will savings rise with the increase in the interest rate. If the response is sluggish, the interest rate must rise by quite a large amount before the desired rise in savings has been achieved. In this case a high rate of subsidies will be required to offset the tendency of the high interest rate to depress investment. It is anticipated that the required rate of subsidies may be so high that the government will find it expedient to turn — at least experimentally — to the course of a budgetary surplus.

*

9. If the government adheres to the course of a balanced budget, it should be helpful if steps are taken to discourage the financing of consumption with bank loans, as discussed in item 7. But restrictions of this kind will be unpopular, and the government may find it more expedient, politically, to rely on a budgetary surplus instead.

*

10. As referred to in Section 12, it has been suggested by Dr. Kuznets that a redistribution of taxes should help in promoting an increased rate of savings. The theory is that if taxes on the relatively rich are reduced and compensated for by increased taxes on the relatively poor, the tendency toward saving will increase, since the rich tend to save a greater proportion of take-home income than the poor. The question, then, is how much will the tendency toward saving increase for each billion dollars per year of taxes that are shifted from the rich to the poor.

For an illustrative study let us assume that: (a) savings for the economy as a whole are 10 percent of take-home income, (b) savings among the people to suffer a tax increase are 9 percent of take-home income, and (c) savings among the people to be favored with a tax cut are 20 percent of take-home income. Assuming that these percentages remain unchanged with a shift in taxes from the richer group to the poorer group, it follows that for a shift of 1 billion dollars per year, savings will increase by approximately 100 million dollars per year, or one-tenth of the shift in taxes.

It may be that the values suggested by this illustration are too pessimistic (they may also be too optimistic). But the illustration does indicate the likelihood that the shift in taxes will have to be many times the desired increase in savings. On the other hand, the budgetary surplus required to produce a given increase in investment should be only fractionally greater than the desired increase. It may be that only experience will prove which course will be less burdensome to the poorer group — they must bear all of the burden of the shift in taxes, or they must bear the bulk of the burden when taxes are raised to provide a budgetary surplus — but it would seem that experiments with shifting taxes will be the poorer risk for them.

SECTION 31

Subsidies on Consumption vs. Subsidies on Investment

It is sometimes believed that subsidies intended to stimulate consumption — such as a reduction of the tax rate on the first income bracket — cannot be relied upon to bring about every upward correction of the aggregate demand that may be required. It is held that in some cases, at least, a concentrated effort must be made to stimulate investment, as through subsidies on investment.

In Chapter VII a number of model cases are employed to illustrate how subsidies on consumption can be effective in every case in raising the aggregate demand in a reasonably satisfactory manner. These models also illustrate how subsidies leading to increased investment will have a similar effect. It is only natural that there should be certain differences in the results of the two approaches, and it may be that some mix of the two approaches will be desirable as a refinement on the policy of employing subsidies on consumption exclusively. But in the larger perspective the subsidies on consumption will give adequate results, and it will be quite practical for the economy to use such subsidies exclusively until experience with control gives clear indications that subsidies on investment are desirable.

The advantage of subsidies on consumption is that they operate with greater speed and certainty than subsidies on investment. Because of this characteristic the government must rely primarily on these subsidies in controlling the aggregate demand. But if events indicate that subsidies on investment may be expedient—for example, if it is found that the economy is obliged to operate with sustained deficit financing—then the government should experiment with diverting subsidies from consumption to investment.

SECTION 32

Probable Behavior of the PSM

The speculation in Section 24 provides a basis for estimating the value of the PSM in the United States in past years. In Chapter VI the value of the PSM has been computed, on the basis of this speculation, for each year of the periods 1902-1913, 1922-1929, and 1953-1962. These were periods in which the economy was fairly prosperous and free from great abnormalities. The values of the PSM for these years serve as an indication of how the PSM may be expected to behave under the controlled state. A summary of the results in Chapter VI, together with certain speculations on the behavior of the PSM under the controlled state, is as follows:

*

1. The grand mean for all yearly values of the PSM in the periods considered was 0.8 percent of aggregate demand. During the period 1902-1913 the mean value of the PSM was 0.9 percent of aggregate demand, and the maximum departure of any yearly value from this mean was 2.0 percent of aggregate demand. But only seldom did the yearly value depart from the mean by more than 1.5 percent of aggregate demand. During the period 1922-

1929 the mean of the yearly values was 1.0 percent of aggregate demand, and the greatest departure of any yearly value from the mean was 2.5 percent of aggregate demand. Again it was seldom that the yearly value departed from the mean by more than 1.5 percent of aggregate demand. During the period 1953-1962 the mean was 0.5 percent of aggregate demand, and the maximum departure was 2.0 percent of aggregate demand. Here too the yearly value seldom departed from the mean by more than 1.5 percent of aggregate demand.

*

2. On the basis of this experience it is speculated for the controlled state that over any moderately long period, such as 10 years, the PSM will have a mean value close to 0.8 percent of aggregate demand. By this is meant that the long-term mean may range from 0.5 to 1.1 percent of aggregate demand, but is not likely to go beyond this range by any significant amount.

*

3. It is speculated for the controlled state that over any moderately long period, such as 10 years, the yearly value of the PSM will seldom depart from the mean for this period by more than 1.0 percent of aggregate demand, and it likely that for practical purposes 1.5 percent of aggregate demand may be regarded as the limit of departure.

SECTION 33

The Potential of Control Subsidies

The question considered at this point is this: Let it be supposed that the United States adopts control at a time when the outlook is quite pessimistic and business has little confidence in the ability of the government to bring about a satisfactory state through the device of reducing the tax rate on the first income bracket. The question then is that of how effective this device may be.

Specifically, let it be supposed that the PSM is 3 percent of aggregate demand, and that Ep is nil. (These conditions would be characteristic of extreme pessimism, quite difficult to explain under the announced intention of the government to drive the aggregate demand to a satisfactory level at all costs.) In addition, let it be supposed that reducing the tax rate on the first income bracket to nil will produce a budgetary deficit at the rate of 8 percent per year. (This is a reasonable assumption on the basis of conditions in 1962.)

Given these assumptions, let it now be supposed that the government does reduce the tax on the first income bracket to nil. Under these conditions the new-muney-rate, which is equal to the budgetary deficit, exceeds the PSM in the amount of 5 percent of the aggregate demand, and in accordance with the earlier speculations the aggregate demand proceeds to rise at a rate near 15 percent per year. This rate of rise should be sufficient to convince business that the government can make good on its guarantee to establish and maintain a satisfactory level of aggregate demand. (As is discussed in Chapter VII, the alignment of the demand with respect to the supply capabilities of the economy should be reasonably satisfactory.)

A natural result of this demonstration would be that the PSM would decline to a value consistent with an optimistic outlook, and the value of Ep would rise in the same way. For example, the PSM might fall to 1 percent of aggregate demand, and Ep might rise to 3 percent of aggregate demand. Then, with the flexible tax at nil, the aggregate demand would rise at a rate near 30 percent per year. This means that the government would have to move rapidly to restore the tax rate on the first income bracket to a more suitable value.

On the more optimistic side, however, it is likely that when the government announces its intention to maintain full control, this in itself will be so powerful a stimulus that no reduction of the tax rate on the first income bracket, or only a modest reduction, will be required. In the long run the government should be able to operate with a balanced budget or even a modest budgetary surplus.

SECTION 34

The Potential of Depressing Ep

In considering the potential of reducing Ep in effecting downward corrections of the aggregate demand, let it be supposed that the desired rate of rise of the aggregate demand is 6 percent per year. Under this assumption, certain cases will illustrate the effectiveness of reducing Ep.

First, let it be supposed that the PSM is minus 1 percent of the aggregate demand. According to the speculations in Section 32, this will be an exceptionally low value. In addition, let it be supposed that Ep has been reduced to zero. With the flexible tax at the normal value there will be a budgetary surplus at the rate of 0.5 percent of aggregate demand. This, together with the fact that Ep is zero, determines that the new-muney-rate is minus 0.5 percent of aggregate demand, so that this quantity exceeds the PSM, algebraically, by 0.5 percent of aggregate demand. According to the earlier speculations this means that the aggregate demand rises at a rate close to 1.5 percent per year. But since the desired rate of rise of the aggregate demand is 6 percent per year, it may be said that the aggregate demand falls with respect to the desired curve at a rate close to 4.5 percent per year. Thus, with the PSM at an exceptionally adverse value, reduction of Ep to zero brings about a fairly rapid downward correction of the aggregate demand.

Secondly, let it be supposed that the PSM is minus 2.5 percent of the aggregate demand, with Ep reduced to zero. Here the new-muney-rate exceeds the PSM by 2 percent of aggregate demand, and the aggregate demand rises at a rate close to 6 percent per year, the desired rate. If the aggregate demand lies above the desired curve, so that a downward correction is required, or if the PSM should fall any lower (become more negative), a supplementary tax program will be required, as discussed in Section 30. But it is held that there is little reason to expect the PSM will ever fall so low as minus 2.5 percent of the aggregate demand.

SECTION 35

Rapidity of Response to the Controls

A question of major importance is that of how rapidly the aggregate demand will respond to application of the control measures. This will determine how closely the government can keep the actual aggregate demand to the desired curve.

This matter is discussed in Chapter VIII. A speculation suggested by the observations there is this: For any full year the volume of aggregate demand will rarely depart from the volume under the desired curve for that year by more than 1.5 percent, and for practical purposes a departure of 2.0 percent may be regarded as the limiting value.

SECTION 36

Government Spending Through Taxes versus Deficit Financing

The principles suggested at this point are these: (1) A program of spending through taxation is relatively ineffective as a pump-priming device. If the controlled economy finds it necessary to operate with sustained deficit financing, and if it seeks to eliminate this with a program of additional government spending through additional taxation, the amount of this program will have to be many times as large as the deficit financing it replaces. (2) The effects of the program referred to in item (1) are not permanent. In time the need for deficit financing will return, as though the program of spending had never been introduced. (3) If the United States were to adopt control, and if it were to cut spending by a large amount, then, after an adjustment period of a number of years, the need for deficit financing (if any) would be no greater than it was before the curtailment in spending.

To study this matter, let it be supposed that the United States has adopted control and that these conditions exist: (a) Ep is 2 percent of the aggregate demand. (b) Deficit financing at the rate of 2 percent of aggregate demand is required in maintaining control. (c) For the sake of reducing the deficit financing the government proposes to increase its spending and taxes by 2 percent of aggregate demand.

Given these conditions we have that the people wish to save muney at the rate of 4 percent of the aggregate demand, or the sum of Ep and the deficit financing. Assuming that Ep remains unchanged, the deficit financing will diminish if the rate of muney-savings is reduced below 4 percent of aggregate demand. The theory behind the contemplated spending program is that, when it is introduced, the rate of muney-savings will fall and this will reduce the deficit financing by an equal amount. But the question is how much will the rate of muney-savings fall, and how lasting will the effect be.

It is suggested that the key to this matter lies in a principle which — when simplified so as to remove complications of secondary importance — may be stated in this way: When there is a sudden decrease in the per capita real take-home income, the rate of muney-savings for the whole economy, as a percentage of take-home income, falls; when there is a sudden increase in the per capita real take-home income, the rate of muney-savings rises; between disturbances of this kind the rate of muney-savings tends to remain a constant percentage of take-home income, and after each such disturbance it settles back to this percentage of take-home income.

Assuming for the moment that this principle is substantially correct, we may observe how it operates in the case under consideration. When the new taxes are applied, per capita real take-home income falls 2 percent. We may assume that as a result of this change the rate of muney-savings falls by one-half the taxes, or to 3 percent of the aggregate demand. This reduces the deficit financing to 1 percent of the aggregate demand.

But now there is another type of development to be considered. This is the natural rise of per capita real take-home income with increases in productivity. For a representative case we may take this as 3 percent per year. Let us then consider the economy 8 months after the introduction of the new taxes, by which time the per capita real take-home income will have been restored to its level prior to the new taxes. It is held that by this time, or shortly thereafter, the rate of muney-savings will have returned to the level that existed prior to the new taxes. The deficit financing required will then be the same as before. After this state has been reached, further increases in the per capita real take-home income, with increasing productivity, will not produce any further increases in the rate of muney-savings.

Let us now examine the validity of the principle stated. It seems that few people will disagree with the claim that a sudden increase or decrease in per capita real take-home income will bring about an increase or decrease in the rate of muney-savings. The objections are likely to come in connection with the claim that any such increase or decrease in the rate of muney-savings must be of a transient nature. Yet the contrary belief leads to an absurdity. The contrary belief is that any increase or decrease in the per capita real take-home income produces a lasting increase or decrease in the rate of muney-savings; and this, in turn, means that increases in the rate of muney-savings with increases in per capita real take-home income must be cumulative. If this were true we should find the rate of muney-savings today much greater than it was, say, at the turn of the century, since per capita real take-home income is so much higher now than it was then. Yet we find that this is not so. Comparing any moderately prosperous period in recent years with any comparable period near the turn of the century, we find that the rates of muney-savings are comparable. From this it must be concluded that the rate of muney-savings does not rise or fall systematically and cumulatively with increases or decreases in the per capita real take-home income, but simply suffers transient disturbances.

If this argument is valid, then it may be said that the behavior of the economy, with regard to the need for deficit financing, is essentially independent of whether taxes and spending are high or low. If it is possible for the economy to operate in the probable mode with high taxes and spending, it should be equally possible for it to operate in this mode when the taxes and spending are low, and vice versa. If a given rate of deficit financing is required with low taxes and spending, the same rate of deficit financing will be required with high taxes and spending.

A question that sometimes arises is that of what would happen in the United States if the government were to find it possible to make a very large reduction in spending and taxes, and proceeded to do so. It is sometimes believed that in this case a large amount of deficit financing would be required to replace the spending eliminated. The theory here is that if the reduction in government spending were quite sudden, a fairly large amount of deficit financing would be required at first as compensation — possibly as much as half the reduction in spending. But this deficit financing would diminish quite rapidly in the beginning, and in time would subside to nil. If the economy was operating in the probable mode to begin with, it should return to the probable mode in time. Or if some rate of deficit financing was required to begin with, in time the required rate of deficit financing should return to a value comparable to that before the reduction in spending.

Some observations of interest may be made in connection with the text-book *Economics: An Introduction to Analysis and Policy,* by Prof. G. L. Bach (second edition). On Page 307, in outlining some current theories, Prof. Bach says the following on the effectiveness of government spending through taxes in boosting aggregate demand: "If the government finances its outlays by collecting taxes, this net addition is doubtful. Most taxes cut into either private investment or consumption, or both — though taxes on the rich in depression may draw funds that would otherwise have lain idle." In effect Prof. Bach is saying what is held here, namely, that (a) a program of additional government spending financed with additional taxes would be effective if the additional taxes did not detract from private spending but rather were defrayed by the taxpayers through a reduction in muney-savings, and (b) the program is ineffective because the taxes do detract from private spending and decrease the rate of muney-savings by only a relatively small amount. But then, on page 279 Prof. Bach says: "Over $70 billion of spending annually by federal, state, and local governments provides a massive, stable component of investment-type spending that can be counted on against any recession tendencies." And on page 255 he says: "But private spending on consumption and investment, plus a steady, solid growth in federal, state and local government spending on public services like roads and schools, have been the biggest factors in the amazing American prosperity of our generation."

It is held that these latter views overestimate the importance of government spending. Also, it would seem that these latter statements are in conflict with the earlier statement of Prof. Bach. Yet there appears to be no discussion of this conflict such as might aim at resolving it.

SECTION 37

Modifications to Policies in Sections 16 and 18 for Imperfect Planning of Taxes and Expenditures

It is assumed for the discussions at this point that the economy desires a balanced budget in the long period. Modifications to the discussions for the case in which the economy desires a budgetary surplus over the long period should be apparent.

It was assumed in Section 16, as a matter of policy, that government spending would always adhere very closely to the budget, and that the tax schedule would provide for a small rate of budgetary surplus when the flexible tax was at the normal value. In Section 18 it was recommended that the normal rate of budgetary surplus — the value with the flexible tax at the normal level — be 0.5 percent of the aggregate demand. However, it is not to be expected that the government will be able to follow these rules precisely, and the question arises as to how the government should proceed when sudden changes in the rate of spending, or poor planning of the tax structure, interferes with strict adherence to these rules.

Let it be supposed that: (a) the policies stated in Sections 16 and 18 are being followed, (b) the tax on the first income bracket is at the normal value, providing for the normal budgetary surplus of 0.5 percent of aggregate demand, (c) Ep is at the normal rate as given by equation 2, (d) there is no need for either an upward or downward correction of the aggregate demand, (e) a sudden need for increased government spending, in the amount of 1 percent of aggregate demand, arises, and (f) when the government spending rises it is not compensated for through an increase in taxes. The result of the increasse in spending is that the budgetary surplus gives way to a budgetary deficit at the rate of 0.5 percent of aggregate demand. In this case the proper course of the government will be to reduce the normal rate of Ep by the amount of the increased spending. This means that equation 1 of Section 18 will still apply, with s now being taken as minus 0.5, and c still being taken as 0.5. So long as this situation continues, the growth of the economy will be lower than it should be, because of the depressed state of Ep, and if the increased government expenditures are expected to continue for a considerable length of time, the government should correct the situation as soon as possible by increasing the tax schedule.

On the other hand, let it be supposed that conditions are as stated in (a), (b), (c) and (d) above, but that there is a sudden decrease in government expenditures, and that this is not compensated for through a reduction of the tax schedule. In this case the proper course of the government is to reduce the tax rate on the first income bracket so as to bring about a budgetary surplus at the rate of 0.5 percent of aggregate demand. With the flexible tax reduced, the budgetary surplus will be the same as it was before the decrease in government spending, and the normal value of Ep will still be as given by equation 2. If this condition persists for an extended period of time, the tax on the first income bracket will be lower than it would otherwise be. The objection to this will be that the people in the lower income brackets will be bearing less than an equitable share of the tax burden, assuming that the tax schedule was set up so that the normal value of the flexible tax would provide for an equitable distribution of taxes. The remedy will lie in changing the tax schedule so as to reduce the rates in all brackets.

The ideal will be to have the tax structure geared to government expenditures so that the tax receipts with the flexible tax at the normal value will always provide for a budgetary surplus at the rate of 0.5 percent of the aggregate demand. It will not be possible for the government to realize this ideal completely, and it will not be necessary that it do so. Proper operation of the controls will enable the government to keep the aggregate demand on the desired curve even though there are departures from the ideal arrangement of taxes. But for other reasons — growth and an equitable distribution of taxes — the tax structure should be revised with sufficient frequency to keep the actual arrangement reasonably close to the ideal.

SECTION 38

Modification to Control Policy for the Budgetary Deficit Mode

It has been assumed for most discussions that the demand for Ep will always be sufficiently brisk to keep Ep at the normally restricted value, with possible rare exceptions. It is a part of the hypothesis that this is likely to be true. But it is also possible that matters will be quite different. For example, it is possible that the demand for Ep will generally be below the value given by equation 2 of Section 18, by an amount that makes deficit financing necessary over the long period, even though the interest rate is usually at the lowest realizable value.

The policy to be employed in a case of this kind may be indicated by an illustration. Let it be supposed that these conditions exist: (a) The tax structure is such that with the flexible tax at the normal value there is a budgetary deficit at the rate of 1 percent of aggregate demand. (b) Most of the time Ep is unrestricted and the interest rate is at the lowest realizable value; only for a small part of the time must Ep be restricted in order to prevent excesses of the aggregate demand. (c) Upward corrections of the aggregate demand are effected by reductions of the flexible tax rate. (d) For at least a large part of the time — say approximately half — the flexible tax is at the normal value.

In this case the central part of policy is the choice of the normal budgetary deficit — the rate of deficit to occur with the flexible tax at the normal value. This should be chosen so that for a large part of the time the flexible tax will be at the normal value, as in condition (d). For the sake of comparison we may assume that the economy chooses, instead, to have the normal budgetary deficit nil. Then, under the remaining conditions assumed, the flexible tax will be below the normal value almost all of the time. This means that the people are likely to resent it when the government raises the flexible tax to the normal value, and the government may have to desist from doing so, in which case the normal value of the flexible tax will be meaningless. (The people should be accustomed to paying the normal value of the flexible tax, and should feel that a reduction is a boon.) It will be far more practical for the government to choose an arrangement under which the normal value of the flexible tax provides for an equitable tax burden on the first income bracket, and under which the flexible tax is at the normal value for a reasonably large proportion of the time.

SECTION 39

Government Expenditures and Taxes

A general rule that may be stated for government expenditures is that these should always be at the minimum level consistent with the normal needs of the nation — national defense, education, welfare, etc. This is to say that extra expenditures should never be undertaken for the sake of regulating the aggregate demand (pump-priming), except, perhaps, in isolated cases for the sake of relieving regional hardships. What the normal needs of the nation are at any time will be a highly subjective matter; decisions will depend in large measure on the personalities among the leadership. But in general any expenditure should be justified on the basis of its immediate merits, not on the basis of its influence in bolstering the aggregate demand.

The general rule for taxes is that tax receipts should always be at the level necessary for control, and the tax structure should be arranged so as to satisfy the requirements discussed in Section 37. The tax receipts will be adjusted, through the flexible tax, so as to keep the aggregate demand on the desired curve, and what these are at any time will be determined by the conditions at hand. But if it is found that the flexible rate is generally far below the normal value, then it should be considered that receipts on the first income bracket are below an equitable level. In this case the tax structure should be revamped by reducing the rates on all income brackets, shifting more of the burden to the first bracket. The sign of a need for a general reduction of the tax schedule will always be that the taxes on the first income bracket are too low.

Let it now be supposed that a sizable amount of deficit financing is required on a sustained basis in keeping the aggregate demand on the desired curve. A question then arises as to whether or not it will be desirable for the government to undertake additional expenditures, as for public works, paying for these with a comparable amount of new taxes. According to pump-priming theory this should, if carried far enough, eliminate the need for deficit financing.

It is held that there is no harm associated with the deficit financing in this case and that the government should not undertake anything so doubtful as a program of additional spending and taxation in an effort to replace it. At best it is likely that the program of additional spending and taxes will have to be several times the amount of deficit financing, placing a needless burden on the taxpayers. At worst, the additional spending and taxes will have no lasting effect at all.

Recently there has been almost universal support in the United States for the principle that taxes have been so high as to stand in the way of a satisfactory level of employment. It is held that if the United States were to adopt control, the 1962 tax schedule would not interfere with maintaining a satisfactory level of aggregate demand. If the 1962 tax schedule proved to be unsuitable, the proper application of the control measures would compensate for it, as discussed in Sestion 37. There would be no difficulty in keeping the aggregate demand on the desired curve. If tax receipts proved to be too high with the flexible tax at the normal value, the flexible tax would have to be held at an inequitably low value, in relation to the normal value, and it would be natural for the government to revise the tax structure to correct this.

But, on the other hand, if the government chose to increase expenditures, presumably for causes important to the well-being of the nation, there would be no reason why the economy should not be able to bear the tax burden imposed by the 1962 schedule. It is held that as far as maintaining a satisfactory level of aggregate demand is concerned, it does not matter how high or how low the level of government spending and taxes may be.

SECTION 40

Refinement of Control Policy for Effects of International Trade

It was assumed in Section 18 that the surplus or deficit in the balance of payments would always be insignificant, and the equations stated there for the normal rate of Ep reflect this assumption. However, let it be supposed that the economy is using equation 2, with the policy implicit in this equation, and that there is a sizable surplus in the balance of payments, *b* percent of aggregate demand. In this case a more suitable value for the normal rate of Ep will be given by the equation

$$\text{Normal rate of Ep} = 0.5 + 0.5Z - b$$

When there is a deficit in the balance of payments, the same equation will apply, but *b* will then be negative.

Given that the normal budgetary surplus is 0.5 percent of aggregate demand, and that the normal rate of Ep is as given by this equation, the new-muney-rate, or (Ep — budgetary surplus + *b*), is normally equal to 0.5Z. This is the same value that would obtain if *b* were nil and the normal rate of Ep were as given by equation 2.

The use of the above equation should be optional with the executive, as is true of equation 2 as well. If the modification represented in this equation is not employed, a large deficit in the balance of payments will lead to increased use of control subsidies, and will contribute toward a budgetary deficit over the long period. A large surplus in the balance of payments, without compensation, will lead to more frequent reductions of Ep in effecting downward corrections of the aggregate demand. (It may be noted that a continuous surplus in the balance of payments, sometimes considered an advantage to the economy, contributes toward a lower growth rate by depressing the mean value of Ep over the long period. The same conclusion may be arrived at through reference to equation 3 of Section 22.)

SECTION 41

REFERENCE LEVEL FOR THE TARIFF-SUBSIDY RATES

The average of the tariff-subsidy rates of all the nations (algebraic values in the event that some are negative) will be taken as a reference level. A question that arises is whether or not this level should have a particular value. For example, it may appear that the reference level should be such as will make the lowest tariff-subsidy rate (algebraic value) zero. Or it may appear that the reference level should be zero, placing many of the tariff-subsidy rates in the negative region.

It is submitted that the value of the reference level is of little importance. Any way the array of rates happens to grow should be satisfactory. However, there may be minor advantages connected with having the reference level at some particular value, and the nations can change the reference level at any time, with some adjustment of the relative values, in seeking such advantages.

How it is that the reference level is of little importance may be explained by means of an illustration involving only two nations, and only two people in each nation. Study will show that the principles illustrated apply equally well for all trade in all nations.

Each week a man in England, who shall be referred to as E-1, sells a bolt of cloth to a man in the United States, U-1, for 100 dollars, or the equivalent in English pounds. Each week a man in the United States, U-2, sells a washing machine to a man in England, E-2, for 100 dollars, or the equivalent in English pounds. To begin with the tariff-subsidy rate in England is nil, and that in the United States is 20 percent; and there are no discriminatory tariffs or subsidies on the goods in question (no tariffs or subsidies other than those imposed by the tariff-subsidy rates).

Under these conditions 100 dollars, or the equivalent, passes from U-1 to E-1 in each week, and the same amount of money passes from E-2 to U-2 in each week, so that the balance of payments on these transactions is neutral. U-1 pays 120 dollars for each bolt of cloth, including the duty, and U-2 receives 120 dollars for each washing machine, including the subsidy.

Now, however, let it be supposed that the reference level of the tariff-subsidy rates is raised so that the tariff-subsidy rate for England becomes 10 percent. Some adjustment of the relative values will be required to compensate for this change, and it will be assumed that the tariff-subsidy rate of the United States is raised to 32 percent. Also, it will be assumed that this change occurs in the prices of all goods for export from the two nations: On all goods for export prices are reduced to 90.9 percent of their former values.

We then find these conditions: E-1 sells each bolt of cloth for 90.90 dollars, and U-2 sells each washing machine for 90.90 dollars, so that the balance of payments on these transactions is still neutral. With the subsidy E-1 receives 100 dollars for each bolt of cloth, as before, and with the duty, E-2 pays 100 dollars for each washing machine, as before. U-1 still pays a total of 120 dollars for each bolt of cloth, and U-2 still receives a total of 120 dollars for each washing machine.

Thus it may be seen that a change in the reference level of the tariff-subsidy rates requires an adjustment of the prices of goods for export, which should come about as a natural process, and an adjustment of the relative values of the tariff-subsidy rates. But when these changes have occurred, the net effects for all parties are the same as if there had been no changes at all.

A formula that may be applied in arriving at the new tariff-subsidy rates, on the basis of the existing rates is

$$T = 0.01\,(100 + t)\,(100 + X) - 100$$

where: T is the new tariff-subsidy rate for any given nation, in percentage points; t is the existing rate for that nation, in percentage points, or the rate preceding the change in reference level; and X is a quantity that is the same for all nations, the selection of which will determine the amount of change in the reference level. After the change in reference level, the prices of all goods for export should be changed in accordance with the formula

$$P = \frac{100}{100 + X} p$$

where P is the price of any type of goods after the change and p is the price before the change.

In the illustration T and t for Unites States are 32 and 20, respectively, while T and t for England are 10 and zero, respectively. The value of X is 10, and the multiplier of p in the above formula is 0.909, or 90.9 percent.

SECTION 42

Unilateral Adoption of the Tariff-subsidy Scheme

The outline of the proposed tariff-subsidy scheme may appear to indicate that it would be necessary for all nations, or at least the larger nations, to adopt the proposed scheme simultaneously. This, however, is not so. If the United States were disposed toward adopting the proposed arrangement, and it could obtain clearance on any conflicts in existing trade agreements, then adoption of this scheme by the United States alone should prove effective in solving the balance-of-payments problem.

Assuming, for example, that the United States were to adopt a tariff-subsidy rate of 10 percent and that this proved to be the proper value for eliminating the current deficit in the balance of payments, the effect on import and export transactions would be the same as if the currency had been devalued by 10 percent.

But to foreign holders of dollars and dollar securities there would be no change.

It is natural that many nations would be apprehensive toward this kind of change, and would be reluctant to give the necessary waivers on existing trade agreements. On the other hand the welfare of the United States is of great importance to most nations of the free world, and on the basis of their attitudes in recent years it would seem that negotiations for their approval would have a good chance for success within a fairly short period of time. Certainly the imposition of a tariff-subsidy rate should be more acceptable to them than a devaluation of the currency. But it also seems likely that negotiations relating to the adoption of the tariff-subsidy scheme for the United States would lead to the adoption of this scheme by many other nations at the same time.

SECTION 43

Elements of Banking, Currency and Government Finance

A number of suggestions and proposals on banking and finance, most of which have been referred to earlier, are as follows:

*

1. As a somewhat academic matter it is suggested that the United States should adopt a uniform currency to replace the present Federal Reserve notes and Treasury certificates. While it should be suitable to have the Federal Reserve issue all currency, all currency should simply say, in effect, "This is lawful money of the United States." There is no reason why the currency should be redeemable in some other form. It is meaningless for Federal Reserve notes to represent themselves as being redeemable in "lawful money," and there is just as little reason for Treasury certificates to be redeemable in silver. The hypothesis also subscribes to the belief that there is no need to impound a sizable portion of the gold reserves of the Treasury as a "backing" for the currency.

*

2. Under the proposed arrangement the principal function of the Federal Reserve will be that of rediscounting the loans and investments of the common banks, in the sense of accepting these as collateral on loans to the common banks.

In general the Federal Reserve will not buy or sell any government securities. The securities it owns will be frozen in its possession. (This means there will be an end to open market operations.) But there will be no limit to the volume of government securities it may rediscount as collateral.

It is assumed that all banks will be eligible for membership in the Federal Reserve System, and that all banks will be subject to its control.

*

3. The rediscount rate, as set by the Federal Reserve, should always be at the minimum level necessary to make the Federal Reserve self-supporting. The Federal Reserve should not attempt to regulate the rate of bank credit expansion through regulation of the rediscount rate.

*

4. The reserves required by the common banks should be determined by the Federal Reserve. The reserve requirements should be at the minimum level necessary for orderly banking operations, as determined by judgment and experience. But no attempt should be made to influence the rate of bank credit expansion through regulation of reserve requirements.

*

5. As has been indicated earlier, it is proposed that the rate of bank credit expansion in private operations be regulated on a quota basis. In any period, such as any month, each bank will be permitted to expand private loans and investments by some percentage of its resources (deposits plus capital). In the simplest arrangement the percentage will be uniform for all banks; but this may be modified in the manner indicated in item 7 below.

*

6. When the demand for Ep is less than the value allowed under the quota, the government will exhort the banks to reduce the interest rate so as to bring about an increase in Ep. Because the welfare of the banks is so closely bound up with the welfare of the economy, it is likely that this will generally be sufficient to bring about any desired decrease in the interest rate, so long as this remains above some hardship level—previously referred to as the lowest realizable rate.

*

7. When the demand for Ep is less than the value allowed under the quota, it is proposed that the Federal Reserve shall, at its discretion, increase the quota of any banks that apply for such increases. This will reward those banks which take the lead in reducing the interest rate and thereby succeed in attracting a volume of business greater than that allowed under the normal quota. Beyond this, the Federal Reserve may set up a formula under which those banks which consistently fall short of their normal quotas will have a lower than normal quota in times when the demand for Ep is brisk. This will tend to promote the kind of competition that should induce a rapid depression of the interest rate when the demand for Ep tends to fall below the level allowed by the quota.

*

8. The allowable value of Ep, and therefore the quota on loans and investments, will be determined by the executive department.

*

9. It was assumed in Section 16 that the volume of government bonds in the hands of individuals other than banks would remain constant, and this assumption was carried through in the discussions thus far. In considering the effects of variation in this quantity, let us make these assumptions: (a) The government wants a balanced budget over the long period and is using equation 2 of Section 18 for the normal value of Ep, the normal budgetary surplus being 0.5 percent of aggregate demand. (b) The surplus or deficit in the balance of international payments is always negli-

gible. (c) The government bonds held by individuals other than banks diminish at a steady rate of n percent of aggregate demand.

It is suggested that in this case the normal value of Ep should be changed to the quantity $(0.5 + 0.5Z - n)$, assuming that n is sizable. Under the given conditions the bank holdings of government bonds increases at a rate equal to (n — budgetary surplus), or $(n - 0.5)$ percent of aggregate demand when the budgetary surplus is at the normal value. Thus with Ep at the revised normal value, and the budgetary surplus at the normal value, the new muney-rate is the sum of $(0.5 + 0.5Z - n)$ and $(n - 0.5)$, or 0.5Z. This is the same as the new-muney-rate obtained through the use of equation 2 when n is zero.

In Section 40 we considered a correction to the normal value of Ep for the effects of a surplus or deficit in the balance of payments. This correction is additive with that considered here. Given that there is a sizable surplus in the balance of payments, b, with all other things as assumed above, the normal value of Ep should be $(0.5 + 0.5Z - n - b)$.

*

10. If deficit financing should be required on a sustained basis, all newly issued government bonds should bear an arbitrarily low interest rate and should be forced upon the banks on a quota basis in the same way that Ep is restricted on a quota basis. It is sometimes held that the sale of government bonds to the banks is more inflationary than selling them to individuals; and therefore it may seem that it would be preferable for the government to issue bonds with a sufficiently high interest rate to attract individuals as purchasers. It is a part of the general hypothesis, however, that with the aggregate demand held at the optimal level, the rate on inflation is independent of whether the bonds are placed with individuals or the banks.

One effect of issuing government bonds with an arbitrarily low interest rate is that it depresses the return to bank depositors in the forms of interest and services. If we assume, for the sake of study, that the interest rate on all new government bonds is zero, all these bonds being placed with the banks, the net effect is that the revenues of the banks per dollar of deposits diminish. This means that the return to depositors, per dollar of deposits, must diminish. It is suggested, however, that this will not be an inequitable or undesirable development.

The deficit financing is required because the people wish to save muney more rapidly than the banks can place funds in private loans and investments. The deficit financing makes it possible for the people to save more muney than the banks are able to place in this way. The reduction in return on deposits occurs because the revenues of the banks from private loans and investments must be spread out over the increased deposits made possible by the deficit financing. This would seem to be equitable. The government issues its bonds to enable the people to have the rate of muney-savings they want; it should not be required to pay the going interest rate on these bonds in order that the people may have the same income on deposits that they would have if the banks were able to place funds in private loans and investments at a rate corresponding to the chosen rate of muney-savings.

In addition, the declining return on deposits may lead some people to save less wealth in the form of muney. This would make for a reduction in the rate of deficit financing required.

On the surface there appear to be no reasons why the government should not make the interest rate on all newly issued bonds, above the amount of redemptions, zero. But it may be that experience, or a more careful analysis of all factors, will indicate some minimum value above zero.

SECTION 44

Theories on Money and Muney

It is the purpose at this point to present a comparison, in barest essentials, between the views in this hypothesis on muney and certain theories on money with which these views may be confused.

One theory is that the volume of money is dominant in determining the level of business activity, activity rising or falling as this volume increases or decreases. In another theory two independent variables, the volume of money and its velocity of circulation, determine the level of business activity.

In contrast with these theories, the views in this hypothesis may be stated in this way:

*

1. The controlling factor in maintaining a satisfactory state of affairs is the rate at which new muney is introduced into the economy (the new-muney-rate). Proper regulation of this factor alone will serve to maintain any desired level of business activity.

*

2. The existing volume of muney has an important influence on the required new-muney-rate at any time. But this factor alone does not determine the required new-muney-rate. Thus, in regulating the level of business activity, attention must focus on the new-muney-rate itself, not on the volume of muney.

*

3. The concept of the velocity of money as an independent variable influencing the level of business activity is one which contributes little toward an understanding of economic processes. A more appropriate concept, but one which is of little significance as an aid to quantitative analysis, is that muney travels in two separate types of flow. In one type of flow there is a constant velocity, or rhythm. A component of this flow is the weekly payment of wages by employer to worker. Another is the periodic payments by the worker to grocer, butcher, landlord, etc. Then, on the other hand, there are the non-rhythmic components of flow. An example of these is a disbursement by a worker, from muney accumulations, for the purchase of an automobile. On the whole this concept is of little use, and deserves no serious attention in analyzing the behavior of an economy. But the same is true of the theory that deals with a variable average velocity of money as a factor influencing business activity.

SECTION 45

The Farm Problem

It is the object at this point to suggest a few elementary principles bearing on the farm problem in the United States.

First, it is submitted that the farm problem is not an integral part of the fundamental problem we are concerned with here — the maintenance of a reasonably satisfactory state for the economy as a whole — any more than say, a public health program is an integral part of the basic problem. If the present manner of dealing with the farm problem were to continue without significant improvement, after control had been adopted, this would not seriously detract from the well-being of the economy.

It is a common notion that the national economy cannot continue in a prosperous state unless the total farm income is at some unique level, commensurate with the gross national product. The implication of this is that farm prices must be such as will make for the proper total farm income. The theory here is that this notion is without substance. Given that a particular level of aggregate demand will provide for a reasonably satisfactory state, this level of aggregate demand can be maintained without difficulty no matter what the total farm income is. It is desirable that farm income be equitable, and this must be a concern of the government, but it is not true that the major complaints of the farm program must be eliminated before the over-all status of the economy can be reasonably satisfactory.

The basic function of the government in the farm program should be that of using government stockpiles of farm products to effect a reasonable degree of price smoothing. This type of operation can be carried out for all of the farm commodities that can be stored for long periods of time.

The basic scheme would be for the government to maintain a stockpile of each commodity capable of being stored over the long period, as it does now, and to peg the price of each commodity by being ready to buy or sell at that price in unlimited quantities. The price of each commodity would be adjusted from time to time, and the objective in regulating the price would be to cause the mean level of the stock in the given commodity to remain substantially constant, or rise slowly to suit the expanding needs of the economy, over the very long period. The aim of the farm program authority should be to keep the price of each commodity highly stable, in the sense of changing slowly over the long period, even though this policy is attended by large fluctuations in the stock of the commodity. The fluctuations in stock will be due to the peculiar uncertainties that beset the farm industry, the same uncertainties that must be dealt with no matter what form the governmental farm program may take.

It may appear on the surface that this scheme is simply the kind of price-fixing that we are seeking to avoid; but any such view overlooks the deeper truth that this scheme provides for an essentially free market. It is true that at any time the price of each commodity is fixed; but the price is not set arbitrarily; the price is adjusted in such way that over the long period it maintains equilibrium between production and the demand by private buyers. (The demand provided by the government over the long period is nil, since the mean level of the government stock remains essentially constant.) Thus, we have what amounts to a free market with price smoothing superimposed. If the government were to continuously increase the mean level of the stockpile (beyond the slow increase necessary to keep pace with the expanding needs of the economy) through an arbitrarily high price, this would be price-fixing in the common sense.

Implicit in what has been said thus far is that under the scheme proposed there would be no attempt by the government to influence the quantity of production in any of the commodities dealt in, through such means as inducing farmers to restrict acreage. Under this arrangement each farmer would be free to produce as he saw fit, and he would be guided in his decisions by the current prices of the commodities stockpiled by the government. If the prices of the stockpiled commodities proved to be so stable that the farmer was assured of insignificant changes over the growing season, this would be ideal, and the aim of the farm program authority should be to approach this ideal as closely as possible.

SECTION 46

Merchandise Inventories

While merchandise inventories are sometimes treated as an independent variable of great importance in the non-controlled economy, they should not be of similar concern under the controlled state. A matter of interest in connection with merchandise inventories, under the controlled state, is their effect on the PSM. Fluctuations in the level of inventories will make for component changes in the PSM, but these are accounted for in the speculations on the probable behavior of the PSM, as stated in Section 32. It is to be expected, of course, that merchandise inventories will be far more stable in the controlled economy than they have been in the non-controlled economy.

The rate of increase of merchandise inventories constitutes a component of the aggregate demand. As this rate — expressed as a percentage of aggregate demand — rises, the percentage of aggregate demand corresponding to the purchase of finished goods by the ultimate users diminishes. This, however, should be of small importance since merchandise inventories grow at a mean rate in the region of 2 percent of all consumption goods sold. (The mean rate in the United States over the past decade has been 1.5 percent.) If merchants and manufacturers should be disposed toward liquidating inventories, the purchases of finished goods by the ultimate users must rise correspondingly. It is likely, therefore, that in times of heavy liquidations of inventories (if there should ever be any) control subsidies will be required to bolster the demand for consumption goods by the ultimate users. In another view it may be said that when merchants and manufacturers are disposed toward liquidating inventories, this contributes toward an increase in the PSM, as is discussed in Chapter IV, and therefore it contributes toward a need for an increase in the new-muney-rate through control subsidies.

CHAPTER III

The observations in this chapter are concerned with certain views in current economic thought relating to the approach of the United States to a controlled status. In some ways the United States is quite close to the type of control proposed. Two developments would reduce the gap between control and the present status to a much lower magnitude. The first of these is the adoption of the scheme of employing a projected aggregate demand curve as a guide in applying the control measures — or some close equivalent — coupled with a commitment of the government to keep the aggregate demand as close as possible to the projected curve. The second is the adoption of a flexible tax structure as a means for controlling the aggregate demand, especially in effecting upward corrections. There are movements in these directions underway, although they are quite feeble at the present time. These and other, related matters are discussed here.

SECTION 1

PLANNING AND CONTROL

Part I

In October of 1961 the President's Council of Economic Advisers announced an approach to planning which in some respects resembled the scheme proposed here. The "project" of the CEA was reported in *Business Week*, of October 14, 1961, under the heading "CEA's model for growth: Economists' projections show how economy would look if it achieved full employment." In the words of the CEA the project was a "full-employment perspective," and, in the words of *Business Week,* it consisted "of a tentative set of projections of how the nation's economy would look if it achieved something resembling full employment in 1963."

Major points of interest in this project of the CEA were these:

*

(1) A table gave the course of the GNP from the second quarter of 1961 through 1963, as required for full employment in 1963. This corresponded to the projected curve of aggregate demand in the scheme proposed here.

(2) The table of projected GNP allowed for a rise in the price index of 1.5 percent from the second quarter of 1961 to 1963. This was in keeping with the outlook proposed here.

(3) Unemployment for 1963 was projected as 3 percent of the work force. Thus the goal referred to as "full employment" was actually a reasonably satisfactory level of employment, as in the concepts of this hypothesis.

(4) The projections of the CEA had no official status. The executive department did not make so bold as to state that these projections were its best estimate of what the course of the GNP should be.

(5) The government did not assume any responsibility for causing the actual level of GNP to follow the projected curve. Instead, Walter Heller, chairman of the CEA, expected that the "announcement effect" of the project would encourage business to increase capital spending plans in such manner as would cause the GNP to behave in the desired manner. On the other hand Chmn. Heller warned that if business proceeded to increase its capital spending plans, and if this did not have the desired effect, business could not expect the government "to help bail you out."

*

By the end of 1962, this project of the CEA was all but forgotten. Yet it was a step toward recognition of the principle suggested here — that for any period in the immediate future there will be some optimal projected curve of aggregate demand, and that the government will have to make it a part of official policy to define this curve and use it as its goal in directing control activities.

A question that arises is that of why this project of the CEA should have been given so little official sanction, and why it should have received so little attention. Possibly the answer lies in the fact that the government had little confidence in its ability to regulate the level of aggregate demand. Clearly it would not be politic for the government to go on record as favoring a particular course of the aggregate demand, and to commit itself to the policy of keeping the aggregate demand on this course, if it felt that it might be ineffectual in fulfilling its commitments.

The question that then arises is: what will be the attitude of the government when it knows that it can control the course of the aggregate demand, without difficulty, with a reasonably high degree of precision? It is suggested that then it will be difficult to explain the position of the government if it fails to commit itself to regulating the aggregate demand in a systematic way. It would be as though the driver of an automobile were to decide that he is not responsible for keeping his vehicle on the road and were to let go of the steering wheel, allowing the vehicle to take whatever course it chose.

But perhaps this analogy of the driverless automobile is not quite appropriate. Let it be supposed that the government knows that it can regulate the aggregate demand in any desired manner, and that instead of keeping the aggregate demand on a predetermined optimal curve it continues with the kind of haphazard control it has been employing for the past decade or more. This is not exactly analogous to a driverless automobile, for there is some measure of control. The government does act in accordance with certain criteria, ill-defined at best, and does make various control decisions, such as inducing a change in the interest rate or changing the rate of government spending. Over any period, these actions control the behavior of the aggregate demand just as surely as would actions designed to keep the aggregate demand on an optimal curve. Thus it is not apt to say that over the given period the economy has behaved like a driverless automobile.

But if we look back over this period and see that the aggregate demand has behaved in an unsatisfactory manner, then we may say that the economy has been controlled in the same way as an automobile in which the driver has deliberately steered through all the ditches in sight; and if control in the economy has prevented major depressions and inflationary booms, the government may be congratulated in the same way that the driver of the automobile may be congratulated for not having collided with any trees.

Part II

In his book *Economics: An Introductory Analysis,* Prof. P. A. Samuelson states, "We shall see that perfectly sensible public and private policies can be followed that will greatly enhance the stability and productive growth of our economic system. They cannot expect to wipe out business fluctuations 100 percent. We would not want them to even if they could. But they can try to reduce the range of wild fluctuations in prices and employment. . . ."

Presumably this must be interpreted a meaning that we should not want control to keep the aggregate demand as close as possible to a stable curve, and that we should set our sights simply on preventing wild departures from the optimal curve. Prof. Samuelson does not say why complete elimination of "business fluctuations" (presumably oscillations about an optimal curve) is undesirable, so one can only guess. One guess is that there is confusion here between strict adherence to an optimal curve and curtailment of the freedom of business. Possibly it is felt that under adherence of the aggregate demand to an optimal curve business, or perhaps even the workers, will lose certain cherished freedoms.

In examining this question of freedom, we may consider an illustrative case that will contrast the major implications of the control scheme proposed here with those of the type of scheme alluded to by Prof. Samuelson. Let it be supposed that as of a given time the aggregate demand has been falling, and that it now lies a small amount below the optimal curve — say 2 percent below. Under the proposed scheme it will be typical for the government to employ fiscal and monetary policies at this point for correcting the unfavorable trend of demand. Under the type of scheme that would meet with the approval of Prof. Samuelson it would be typical for the government to defer action until the demand had fallen to a much lower level—such as 6 percent below the optimal level—and then the government would be required to use fiscal and monetary policies to correct the unfavorable trend of demand. In these two types of treatment we have the distinction between freedom and the lack of it. When the controls are applied clumsily and adjusted infrequently, so as to permit relatively large excursions of the aggregate demand from the optimal curve, we have freedom. And when the same controls are applied skillfully and adjusted frequently, so as to keep the aggregate demand always close to the optimal curve, we have a lack of freedom. In the same way one should expect that if all the carefully timed traffic lights in New York City were to lose synchronism and begin to operate in a somewhat helter-skelter fashion, there would be more freedom for traffic than now exists. But in such matters as the freedom of the individual businessman to run his business as he chooses, it is difficult to discern any difference under the two types of scheme.

Part III

At present control in the United States is predominantly a matter of (a) "putting on the brakes" when the aggregate demand is rising and alarming signs of inflation appear, and (b) opening the throttle wide when the economy is in a depressed state and the inflationary pressures have subsided.

In the early part of 1961, the economy was in a depressed state. The new administration promptly initiated measures to bring about a rise in activity. Shortly after the ensuing rise had begun, the administration became alarmed at the signs of inflation and then proceeded to put on the brakes. Whether because of the brakes or other causes, the improvement in employment came to a halt, and the economy continued in a depressed state through 1961 and 1962. This sequence demonstrates the difficulties that face us when we try to correct a recession by opening the throttle and crossing our fingers in the hope that excessive inflation will not attend the rise in activity.

In the early part of 1963 plans in the United States called for a reduction in taxes for the purpose of bringing about an upsurge in activity. Assuming that the sought-for rise does occur, it remains to be seen how soon alarming signs of inflation will appear, and whether or not the government will again find it expedient to put on the brakes before unemployment has been reduced to a reasonably satisfactory level. But most important is that the plans do not anticipate the occurrence of intolerable inflationary pressures, and they do not provide in advance for the course of action to be followed if such forces do appear.

In contrast, under the proposed scheme the aggregate demand would be advanced at a predetermined rate, with a specific allowance for the rate of inflation. If the rate of inflation should rise above the value allowed for, there would be no deviation from the predetermined course of the aggregate demand. It would simply be made clear to labor and business that their inflationary pressures were detracting from the planned improvement in employment. Each year the allowance for inflation and improvement in employment (the planning cushion) would be adjusted in accordance with developments, and in time the economy should settle out to a fairly stable compromise between the rate of inflation and the level of unemployment. This scheme would not be an open sesame to a completely satisfactory state. Its advantage over the scheme of alternately opening the throttle and putting on the brakes, as the spirit moves the guiding powers, would lie in the greater orderliness and stability it would provide for, together with the improved atmosphere for the development and operation of the forces of moral suasion.

Part IV

The New York Times of 20 February 1962 reported a plan for fighting slumps, proposed by the President, that represented a small step in the direction of applying the control devices in accordance with the formula approach. Highlights of the President's proposals, submitted to Congress on 19 February were: (1) A fund of 2 billion dollars was to be placed at the President's disposal to be used for public works in accordance with a rigid formula, based on the percentage of unemployment. (2) The formula contained terms such as: public works would be initiated "when the national unemployment rate, adjusted for seasonal factors, had risen in three out of four, or four out of six consecutive months."

Plainly this proposed arrangement was not intended to cover all control operations, but only one small segment of the over-all control scheme. Presumably, if this plan showed merit, it would be extended to other control operations, and we may examine it from the point of view of how it would apply if it were extended to all control operations.

The major criticism is that this plan simply provides a specific criterion for opening the throttle; it does not provide criteria for determining how much the throttle should be opened, and it does not anticipate actions to be taken if the forces of inflation, induced by an upward movement of activity, should become excessive. The plan is based on the level of unemployment, and presumably increased spending would continue until unemployment had been reduced to a satisfactory level. But it must also be presumed that if alarming signs of inflation appeared before a satisfactory level of employment had been reached, the answer to this development would simply be to put the brakes on, as in the past.

Part V

A search of *The Report of the Commission on Money and Credit* for recommendations concerning systematic planning and control reveals what may be paraphrased in these terms: (1) Whenever the President feels the trend of the economy is moving significantly counter to the objectives set forth in the Employment Act he shall make this known in a special report to Congress. The first report for any given unfavorable trend shall be followed quarterly by additional reports on progress in dealing with the given situation. (2) The report shall set forth what the executive department is doing with the means subject to its control. (3) The report shall make recommendations for congressional action deemed advisable.

This is just a way of saying that the economy should continue with the expedients of opening the throttle and applying the brakes, with perhaps somewhat more responsibility for the President in deciding when the time is ripe for action in one direction or the other.

SECTION 2

MONETARY POLICY

Part I

Policy relating to the rate of new muney issue and the interest rate must be tailored to suit the internal needs of the economy; there must be no deviation from this course because of international developments such as an efflux of short-term investment funds from the given economy. The rate of new muney issue must be such as will keep the aggregate demand on the desired curve, and the interest rate must be commensurate with this rate of muney issue; if the optimal interest rate contributes to an unfavorable movement of short-term investment funds, this situation must be corrected by means other than compromising with the interest rate.

Various means of dealing with an unfavorable movement of short-term investment funds are available. If the movement is steady, it may be compensated for through adjustment of the tariff-subsidy rate. If there is a large efflux of foreign-held funds from the given economy because of the interest rate, this may be dealt with, at least in some cases, by adding a differential to the interest rate on foreign-held funds, the cost of the differential being born by the government. An efflux of funds held by nationals of the given economy may be discouraged through taxes on the foreign investments of these nationals. But more generally, troublesome flows of investment funds can be prevented through appropriate barriers and inducements, applied unilaterally or through international cooperative effort. It will be desirable that there be international harmony with regard to these barriers and inducements, and when the nations recognize that it is for their common benefit to prevent disruptive flows of investment funds, the problem of arriving at amicable control arrangements should be one of the lesser problems facing the community of nations.

In September of 1962 Robert Roosa arguing against barriers to the free flow of investment funds stated that such barriers "would literally congeal the bloodstream of American capitalism." The answer to this type of view is one that applies, in sense, in all such cases. The proper medicines, used in the proper proportions, will keep the bloodstream of American capitalism functioning in the best possible way, both in domestic affairs and in international affairs. The medicines can be quite harmful to the bloodstream of American capitalism if they are used improperly, but it will be equally harmful if they are not used at all, as urged by Mr. Roosa.

Part II

Prof. Milton Friedman, in his book *Capitalism and Freedom,* has proposed an arrangement under which the Federal Reserve would be required by law to increase the muney of the economy at a fixed rate, somewhere in the region of 3 to 5 percent of the total muney per year. (It is of interest to note that Prof. Friedman prefers to think of money as including time deposits.) This scheme is similar in some respects to that proposed here, but there are certain significant differences.

Under the policy stated in Section 18 of Chapter II, the economy will normally keep the new-muney-rate at a fixed level, as proposed by Prof. Friedman. But this rate will be changed from time to time in effecting control. For upward corrections of the aggregate demand the new-muney-rate will be increased through control subsidies, and for downward corrections of the aggregate demand the new-muney-rate will be reduced through more stringent restriction of Ep.

Another difference lies in the fact that this hypothesis is more specific, quantitatively, with regard to the new-muney-rate that shall normally be maintained. The proposal here is that the new-muney-rate shall normally be 0.5 times the rate of rise of the projected aggregate demand curve, where the new-muney-rate is in percent of aggregate demand, and the rate of rise of the aggregate demand is in percent per year. For example, if the aggregate demand is 600 billion dollars per year and is required to rise at the rate of 6 percent per year, the new-muney-rate should normally be 3 percent of 600 billion dollars per year, or 18 billion dollars per year. Experience may indicate the desirability of changing the coefficient 0.5 somewhat, but this value should give adequate results until it is clear that there will be an advantage in altering it. This is discussed in Chapter VI.

Part III

Confusion in the matter of monetary policy versus inflation is highlighted by some statements of William McChesney Martin, chairman of the Federal Reserve Board, as reported in an article in The New York Times of 27 August 1962. In this hypothesis it is held that monetary policy cannot contribute to inflation so long as it is employed to keep the aggregate demand at the optimal level. On the one hand the statements of Mr. Martin run counter to this thesis, and on the other hand they contradict themselves.

A few weeks prior to 27 August 1962 it was anticipated that additional deficit financing would be required, and there was a question as to whether the government bonds should be placed with private investors or sold to the banks. Mr. Martin was understood to be in opposition to placing the bonds with the banks on the grounds that this would be inflationary. In this connection he said "we must not finance a deficit by bank-created funds."

Subsequently, testifying before the Joint Economic Committee of Congress, Mr. Martin stated that there was nothing wrong with selling the Government bonds to the banks as long as individuals placed their savings with the banks. In this case, said Mr. Martin, the deficit "is being financed by real savings just as surely as if the individuals had purchased savings bonds in the first instance."

It seems reasonable to believe that as a general rule individuals do place the bulk of their money-savings in the banks, and if this is accepted as true, then it follows that Mr. Martin is in agreement with the principle that placing Government bonds with the banks is no more inflationary than selling them to individuals. It seems unfortunate, however, that Mr. Martin's logic had to follow so devious a route in leading to this conclusion. While the conclusion is in agreement with this hypothesis, it is not clear that the logic is equivalent in the two explanations.

Part IV

Some points of interest in the matter of the best interest rate for internal affairs, together with the matter of the best interest rate for international affairs, are highlighted by testimony before the Joint Economic Committee of Congress, as reported by The New York Times of 17 August 1962. The testimony was given by Mr. Martin, chairman of the Federal Reserve Board, and Alfred Hayes, president of the Federal Reserve Bank of New York.

Both men agreed that there was need for the economy to perform better than it had been performing. But it was implied that monetary policy had been used to do all that could be expected of it. Mr. Hayes stated: "The job of instilling new vigor into the business expansion must, I believe, be done largely by means other than monetary policy." Both men indicated opposition to a reduction of the interest rate.

It is held in this hypothesis that the most important step in establishing and maintaining a satisfactory state is the formal adoption of control of the type proposed. Only after control has been adopted will the economy be able to determine the best level for the interest rate. In view of this it is not appropriate to criticize the statements of Mr. Martin and Mr. Hayes directly. But let it be supposed that control has been adopted and that conditions are then as they were when Mr. Martin and Mr. Hayes gave their testimony. In this case there would be no justification in the stands taken by both men. With the rate of bank credit expansion to private borrowers lagging, as it was in 1962, there would be no justification in opposing a reduction in the interest rate.

Both Mr. Martin and Mr. Hayes indicated that there was a danger in reducing the interest rate because of the possibility of an outflow of investment money from the economy. It is held that this should never be a consideration in adjusting the interest rate; other means should be employed in dealing with problems of this kind.

At one point Mr. Martin said that the economy had not yet come to the point of conflict where a reduction in the interest rate would be desirable for internal affairs but inadvisable because of the possibility of an efflux of investment funds. Again it is not apppropriate to criticize this against the background of the non-controlled economy. But let it be supposed once more that control has been adopted and that conditions are as they were at the time of the testimony. Here it will be plain that a reduction of the interest rate is required. And if this will lead to an efflux of investment funds, the economy then does stand at the crossroads of conflict between domestic and international goals. The proper course will be the reduction of the interest rate and special measures for controlling the investment funds.

SECTION 3

Flexible Taxes, Tax Cuts, Tax Reform

Part I

A flexible tax rate on the first income bracket, subject to the control of the executive department — or some close equivalent — will be an indispensable element of control. This will be a powerful device for driving the aggregate demand upward when control is adopted, assuming that the aggregate demand is at a depressed level to begin with, as discussed in Section 33 of Chapter II. After the demand has been driven to the optimal level, this device will be a powerful means by which the government can exert continuously variable control in keeping the aggregate demand on the desired curve.

It appears that the only serious objections to the proposed arrangement derive from the view that under this arrangement the Congress would be surrendering its Constitutional and traditional control over taxes, with an intolerable weakening of the principle of checks and balances in our government. (Attention is invited to the opinion of Charles B. Shuman in the Report of the CMC, page 129.) It is suggested, however, that when all of the elements of the scheme proposed in this hypothesis are taken into consideration, this objection loses much of its force.

Under the proposed scheme, the Congress determines the optimal course of the aggregate demand, it sets up a normal tax schedule, and it delegates the President to vary the tax on the first income bracket (within the range below the normal level) in such manner as he sees fit for the purpose of keeping the aggregate demand on the desired curve. A further provision implicit in the arrangement is that the President is under obligation to aim at keeping the budget balanced over the long period, unless the Congress has set up the tax schedule in a manner designed to provide a budgetary surplus over the long period, in the interest of accelerated growth. In either case the intentions of the Congress will be made known to the President, and he will be under obligation to regulate the controls in a manner that will comply with this intent through policies such as those outlined in Chapter II.

It is suggested that in view of these elements of the proposed scheme it is hardly proper to take the view that the Congress will be surrendering its authority over tax matters to the President. A more reasonable view is that the Congress will simply be translating its authority into another form — a form under which the President is delegated to vary taxes in accordance with its intent.

It was suggested in Chapter II that it might be satisfactory to employ an arrangement under which the executive department would establish the desired curve of aggregate demand. This would, of course, weaken the system of checks and balances, and would be objectionable to those who prefer the present division of power between the Congress and the President.

Part II

In the early part of 1962 the President asked Congress for standby authority to reduce income taxes temporarily at his discretion. This would have been a major step in the direction of a flexible tax structure as recommended by the Commission on Money Credit. When this request was denied, the efforts of the administration at securing a flexible tax structure collapsed. Subsequently the administration made a complete about-face. In the late part of 1962 it appeared that Congress was amenable to a temporary tax cut, as urged by many leaders in all sectors of the nation. At this point the administration became contemptuous of a "quickie" tax cut, as it was referred to by the President in his address of 14 December 1962, and insisted that only a permanent tax cut would satisfy the needs of the economy.

It is suggested that this change in the outlook of the administration was an unfortunate one. What is needed most, for now and the future, is a flexible tax structure. A temporary tax cut would be a step in the direction of a flexible tax structure. Insisting upon a permanent tax cut is a step in the opposite direction.

If a temporary tax cut were to be enacted, the implication would be that the tax cut could be rescinded, either wholly or partially, on short notice. This would prepare the way for increases and decreases of taxes on short notice as a general rule.

As of the early part of 1963 it appeared that a permanent tax cut was preferred over a temporary one only for the sake of tax reform. It appeared that those who advocated the permanent tax cut, in preference to the temporary one, did so only because they felt that this was the best way to achieve cherished reforms. If it were not for the reforms, there could have been no objection to the temporary cut, or no reason for holding out for a more binding arrangement.

From a scientific viewpoint, as distinguished from a political one, it is held that this outlook is appropriate in the matters of tax cuts and reforms: (a) Tax reform should be treated separately from the matter of changing the general level of taxes. (b) The economy should proceed as rapidly as possible to the type of flexible taxes proposed by the CMC, as enlarged upon in this hypothesis; but as an interim arrangement the economy would do well to have a flexible tax structure such as would be provided by temporary tax cuts, with short-notice restorations, through Congressional action. (c) There is no need for haste on tax reforms. These should, of course, be made whenever it is clear that they are desirable or expedient. But reforms will be of secondary importance, compared with flexible taxes, as a means for establishing and maintaining a satisfactory level of aggregate demand. Moreover, it is likely that as the economy moves more in the direction of control, it will be in a better position to see what direction reforms should take. Therefore reforms should be deferred until the effects of flexible taxes have been observed. Reforms may be helpful for such purposes as stimulating investment, but they should be regarded as a refinement in the control scheme rather than a prime mover.

Part III

During the latter part of 1962 it was almost a fad for economists and others to speak of the taxes in the United States as being too high. In most instances it was claimed that high taxes were responsible for the lag in activity during the Kennedy administration, and that the tax structure constituted an insuperable obstacle to prosperity. Perhaps the most weighty pronouncements of this kind were those in the address of the President on 14 December 1962 and the policy statement of the Committee for Economic Development of December 1962.

It is held that if the United States were to adopt control, with the 1962 tax structure, but with the tax on the first income bracket flexible, there would be no difficulty in bringing the aggregate demand to a satisfactory level and keeping it there. There would be nothing about the 1962 tax structure to stand in the way of this.

It has been estimated that if the aggregate demand were at a satisfactory level, the tax receipts under the 1962 schedule, with the flexible tax at the normal value, would exceed government expenditures by a wide margin—in the region of 2 percent of the aggregate demand. Given that this is so, one possible effect is that the tax on the first income bracket would have to be kept far below the normal value in maintaining control. The objection to this would be that the people in the lower income brackets were bearing less than an equitable share of the tax burden; the remedy would be a reduction of the rates on all brackets so as to shift part of the burden from the upper brackets to the lowest bracket. This would in some measure vindicate the claims that the 1962 tax structure was too high.

But there are other possibilities to be considered, and if the United States were on the verge of adopting control, these would argue in favor of deferring a general reduction in taxes until events had clarified matters. The first of these possibilities is that: (a) control has been adopted with the 1962 tax structure, and the tax receipts with the flexible tax at the normal value provide for a current budgetary surplus at the rate of 2 percent of the aggregate demand, (b) the government and the people want the budgetary surplus provided by the maximum tax receipts for the sake of accelerated growth, and (c) the demand for Ep is sufficiently great to enable the government to keep the tax receipts at the maximum level. In this case the 1962 tax schedule will have proved to be just right as far as total tax receipts is concerned. There may, of course, be arguments favoring tax reforms, but this will be a matter apart from the general level of taxes.

A second possibility is that conditions are as stated in (a) above, but that there is a strong desire for increased government expenditures for causes important to the well-being of the nation, and that to satisfy these desires the government brings expenditures into balance with the maximum tax receipts. Here again the 1962 tax schedule will have proved to be just right. It must be recognized that in recent years there has been some measure of penny-pinching on government expenditures, because of slack tax receipts, and it is entirely possible that when tax receipts improve there will be strong demands for increased government spending to match.

The most objectionable feature of the arguments favoring a permanent tax cut is the specious claim that high taxes have been responsible for the lag in activity in recent years. This is another attempt to attach a functional cause to a recession, or lag in activity, when it seems so much more probable that the difficulties should be explained in terms of psychosomatic behavior. It is held that the lag in investment in recent years has been due to a lack of optimism such as would be corrected by the adoption of control. So long as psychological factors are free to dominate the course of investment—so long as it is a part of the scheme of things for the President's Council of Economic Advisers to warn business that it cannot expect the government to bail them out if the aggregate demand fails to keep pace with their investment programs—there can be no justification for seizing upon one functional factor or another, such as the tax structure, in explaining a lag in investment. It is held that the behavior of the economy is essentially independent of the general level of taxes and government expenditures, as discussed in Section 36 of Chapter II. If the United States were to reduce taxes and expenditures to the level preceding the Great Depression, while retaining the non-controlled state, the economy would then be no less susceptible to lags in investment than it has been in the past few years.

It is suggested that the present corporate income taxes are in no way a deterrent to investment. In highly prosperous years of the past decade, particularly 1955 and 1957, business has indicated that it is quite eager to expand productive capacity when there is a promise of ample markets for its products, even though it must pay up to 50 percent of its profits in taxes. The 50 percent retained is still an inducement to increased earnings through increased sales.

Moreover, a reduction in corporate income taxes is not likely to bring about an increase in returns on investment. In the present scheme of things income taxes are treated as a cost. Profits before taxes are not regarded as profits any more than profits before payroll payments are regarded as profits. The all-important issue is profits after taxes, and pricing policies aim at a reasonable return in this respect. If corporate income taxes are lowered, it is to be expected that competition will drive prices down, in the same way as it drives prices down when any element of costs is reduced, and the new return should be little different from that preceding the tax reduction.

SECTION 4

International Trade

Part 1

If the nations of the world were to adopt the proposed tariff-subsidy arrangement, competition for foreign markets would still be a vital force in international trade. It is not to be thought that negotiations over discriminatory trade barriers and inducements would be free of discord, as may seem to be implied in the discussions in Chapter II. What is implied is that there would be more room for sportsmanship in these negotiations.

This may, perhaps, be made plainer by an analogy. Let it be supposed that a fire has started in a modern theater and that the audience is aware of this and has been directed to leave. At the same time, in some remote part of the world, a fire starts in a theater which by modern standards is an extremely bad fire-trap. In both cases there will be some measure of competition among the people in getting to the exits. But the behavior of most people in the former case will, to outward appearances at least, be more generous and sportsmanlike than in the latter case. The characteristics of the people may be the same in both cases, but the difference will be that in the former case the people can afford to be more magnanimous. It is suggested that in the same way the tarff-subsidy arrangement will be conducive to greater magnanimity than is possible under the present arrangements and outlook.

Part II

The slogan "Trade or Fade" appears to represent two specious notions which stand in the way of a proper understanding of the problems of foreign trade. The first of these is that when there is an across-the-board lag in activity in a given economy, foreign markets should be sought as a remedy for the situation. The second, closely related to the first, is that the given economy must continuously strive for an across-the-board expansion of its foreign trade in order to provide for its present and future prosperity. The theory involved appears to be the same as that expressed by Walter Lord in his book *The Good Years* when in speaking of China at the turn of the century he said: "Here was the market America needed when she could no longer absorb her own production." At the present time it is not China that America looks to, but, rather, the Common Market of Europe. It may not be fitting to imply that this theory has a high-ranking place in current economic thought; it may be that most economists recognize that this theory is specious. But if this is so, there has been a great laxity in correcting the false impressions of the lay public. Beyond this, it appears quite possible that the false impressions involved do play some part in the policy-making on international trade.

When there is an across-the-board lag in activity the basic fault lies with internal policy. The aggregate demand is too low, and internal policies must be revised so as to bring the aggregate demand up to the optimal value. When the aggregate demand has been brought to the optimal level, there will no longer be an across-the-board lag in activity, but, as a general rule, there will be lags in some sectors of the economy.

Given that most nations have adopted some effective form of control, with the aggregate demand held at the optimal level, each will be troubled with scattered lags in activity. (In the smaller, less diversified economies these may be so acute that it will be inappropriate to refer to them as scattered.) It is here that international trade agreements can be used to best advantage. In general, the optimal distribution of world trade can do a great deal toward relieving the scattered lags in activity in the several economies, and the nations must direct their trade negotiations toward this end for their common benefit. Thus there is little to be said for the view that each nation should seek to expand its foreign trade in all directions; the nations should seek to channel trade along the best routes; and where a need for expansion is indicated, this will be along certain particular routes, and in particular quantities. If the United States and the Common Market have excessive capacity to produce agricultural products, they should not expend their energies in trying to sell agricultural products to each other. The proper course will be to pursue trade agreements under which the agricultural products of these economies will be directed to nations having a deficiency of these goods, and under which the given economies will receive goods for which there is a brisk demand in these economies, when the aggregate demand is at the optimal level.

Part III

One of the current views is that the United States, or any other economy, does not have a free hand in using internal policies for achieving the optimal aggregate demand because of complications with international balances of payments. In his address of 14 December 1962, President Kennedy, speaking of the matter of raising the aggregate demand said: "In the past this could be done in part by the increased use of credit and monetary tools — but our balance-of-payments situation today places limits on our use of these tools for expansion."

The argument in this hypothesis is that by means of the tariff-subsidy arrangement proposed, together with special barriers and inducements relating to movements of short-term investment funds, each economy can separate the problem of maintaining the optimal level of aggregate demand from that of maintaining a satisfactory balance of international payments, placing them in isolated, non-conflicting areas. The tariff-subsidy scheme should be quite powerful in regulating the balance of payments — being capable of doing all that flexible currencies can do, without the difficulties encountered with flexible currencies — and might make regulation of the movements of short-term investment funds unnecessary. Only if the movements of short-term investment funds become highly disruptive surges will it be necessary for a given nation to take unilateral action, or seek international cooperation, in regulating these movements.

In the United States the present administration leans toward the view that control of the flow of short-term investment funds is undesirable. It may be that restraint in this type of control will be best, and that the government should go to great lengths to compensate for unfavorable movements of investment funds through the tariff-subsidy arrangement. But there can be no excuse for allowing unfavorable movements of short-term investment funds to interfere with the objective of maintaining the optimal level of aggregate demand. If such movements cannot be compensated for through the tariff-subsidy arrangement, because of their magnitude or erratic nature, the proper course will be that of regulation. To reject regulation as the appropriate course in these circumstances would be as whimsical as to reject the principle of using traffic lights for the purpose of regulating the flow of vehicular traffic.

Part IV

Against the possibility that the United States may find it necessary to prevent a disruptive efflux of short-term investment funds, two expedients suggest themselves. First, with regard to funds owned by its nationals, the government may apply taxes on foreign-held investments in appropriate amounts. Then, with regard to investments held by foreigners, the government may pay a bonus interest rate (an additional rate above that provided by the securities held) to foreigners.

Assuming that the government is paying out a sizable amount of money to foreigners as a bonus on their investments, and assuming that the situation gives indications of continuing indefinitely, the question arises as to whether or not there is a remedy for this. The answer is that the United States should adopt policies that will provide for the gradual withdrawal of the foreign-held investments until these have been reduced to the point where bonus payments are no longer necessary. For example, let it be supposed that the government adjusts the bonus payments so that foreign-held short-term investment funds diminish at the rate of 1 billion dollars per year. Under the tariff-subsidy arrangement the economy will be able to tolerate this kind of withdrawal. Then, within a fairly short period of time — such as 5 to 10 years — foreign-held investment funds should be at the level where no bonus payments will be required to prevent further efflux.

SECTION 5

Growth Rate

Part I

In recent years there has been a growing tendency to blame our economic ills on a lagging growth rate. Since growth rate is virtually synonymous with the rate of investment, it is suggested that this approach is largely a play on words, sometimes bordering on intellectual dishonesty, and should be discouraged.

To illustrate, let it be supposed that in some garret we come upon a child who is emaciated and of abnormally small size due, as investigation reveals, to years of extreme malnutrition. If in this case we summarize the difficulty by saying that the child has been suffering from a low growth rate, this will be quite true and at the same time closely analogous to saying that the difficulties in our economy, in times of high unemployment, are due to a low growth rate. A news accounts of the incident might read: "An emaciated boy 10 years old and only 3 feet tall was found today in a garret in the . . . section of New York City. Doctors who examined the boy concluded that he was suffering from a lagging growth rate. Further investigation revealed that extreme malnutrition over the past 3 years was a major cause of the condition observed. This is the third similar case of lagging growth rate among children discovered in the . . . area within the past year."

On the surface there is nothing wrong with all of this except for some redundancy in needlessly bringing in the notion of growth rate. But it is suggested that this is dangerous in that it serves as an opening-wedge for confusion in the line of thought between cause and effect. We have been in a recession in recent years because business has lacked the optimism necessary for a satisfactory rate of investment—the kind of optimism that could be brought about through control of the aggregate demand. But let some economists keep pounding away at a lagging growth rate as the cause of our economic ills, and from there it is just a short step to picking causes of the lagging growth rate out of a hat. It is suggested that this kind of process has occurred in associating the 1962 tax structure—now referred to sometimes as that nasty war-time tax structure—with the lagging growth rate. It is held that no case has been made for blaming the lag in investment in recent years on the 1962 tax structure. There is no reason to believe that the economy would be less susceptible to lags in investment under some other tax structure. But it is a fad to blame the lag in investment on a lag in growth rate (even though the two are synonymous), and when one is ready to subscribe to this fad he is also ready to subscribe to the fad of believing that recent taxes have been too high for the existence of a satisfactory state.

It would have been proper in the days of the Great Depression to have spoken of our difficulties in terms of a lagging growth rate, but this would have added nothing but confusion to the situation. It adds nothing but confusion now to speak of the recent high level of unemployment in terms of a lagging growth rate.

Part II

Assuming that the United States has adopted control and that a sizable volume of deficit financing is required over the long period in maintaining control, it will then be true that investment is not up to the level made possible by the rate of savings. In this case it will be meaningful to say, alternatively, that the growth rate is lower than that made possible by the rate of savings, and it will be constructive for the government to use the notion of improved growth rate in justifying measures aimed at stimulating investment. But this will be meaningful only in an atmosphere of control — where there is a guarantee that the aggregate demand will be kept at the optimal level. A similar kind of meaning does not obtain under similar circumstances in the non-controlled economy, since psychosomatic behavior can play so large a part in depressing the rate of investment. Where a child's growth is stunted by extreme malnutrition, it makes little sense to think in terms of growth rate; but where a child is living under normal conditions and is believed to be suffering from a growth-retarding glandular ailment, then it is reasonable to think in terms of growth rate.

A great question that exists is whether or not deficit financing on a sustained basis will be required if the United States adopts control. Implicit in the views of the President, as stated in his speech of 14 December 1962, is that deficit financing will be required if the 1962 tax structure is retained. On the other hand the views of Dr. Kuznets in *Capital in the American Economy: Its Formation and Financing* suggest that deficit financing will not be required. This hypothesis holds that the recent lag in investment has been due to psychosomatic behavior, like all preceding lags in investment, and if control should be adopted it is highly unlikely that net deficit financing will be required over the long period. Moreover, it is held likely that the economy will be able to maintain a moderate budgetary surplus, if it so chooses, in the interest of accelerated growth. If the 1962 tax structure should provide for a budgetary surplus under the optimal level of aggregate demand, as has been estimated, it is entirely possible that under the controlled state the demand for Ep will be sufficiently brisk to support this.

Whether or not the economy should strive for an accelerated growth rate will be a highly subjective matter. One reward will be greater prestige and power for the United States in world affairs. Another will be greater future benefits for the people of the nation. The disadvantage of an accelerated growth rate is that the people must accept a lower present rate of consumption than they might otherwise have.

SECTION 6

INFLATION

Part I

In a speech on 27 September 1962, Mr. Allan Sproul, former president of the New York Federal Reserve Bank said, in effect, that inflation must be cured at the bargaining table in arriving at wage pacts, and that fiscal and monetary policies are of little help in suppressing the forces of inflation. These views summarize the position of this hypothesis on the causes of inflation. But the problem of inflation cannot be dealt with on the level of the bargaining table alone, as the remarks of Mr. Sproul suggest.

The economy must rely primarily on the course of compromise between inflation and unemployment through planning of the aggregate demand. With this scheme in operation, moral suasion can play a large part in suppressing the inflationary pressures at the bargaining table and thus bring about a higher level of employment for any rate of inflation that may be tolerated. But it must be recognized that moral suasion must also be brought to bear on pricing policies, as well as wage bargains, for we cannot expect labor to yield to moral pressures unless business sets a good example in this respect.

Moral suasion will become increasingly effective as society develops a code of fair practices in the matters of wage rates and pricing policies — one that is subscribed to by an impressive part of the leadership in all sectors of society.

Part II

In his speech of 14 December 1962 President Kennedy noted that inflation had "been arrested," and indicated that no further problems with inflation were to be expected. Speaking of the prospect of "full employment," to be achieved through his proposed tax revisions, the President said: "It will not, I am confident, revive an inflationary spiral or adversely affect our balance of payments. If the economy today were operating close to full employment, or if a sudden change in our military requirements should cause a scramble for men and resources, then I would oppose tax reductions as irresponsible and inflationary."

It is suggested that this outlook does not have a proper respect for the forces of inflation that tend to develop as employment approaches a satisfactory level, and that it leads to policy that is as improvident as that of the ostrich in burying its head. The forces of inflation have been quiescent in recent years because of the relatively high level of unemployment. As employment rises these forces will spring back with great vigor. Policy should be prepared to deal with them in a systematic manner. But if there should be a rise in employment, and if this should bring on a serious rise in the forces of inflation, as anticipated in this hypothesis, it is likely that the administration will meet this by simply putting on the brakes, as it met a similar situation in the past.

Part III

On 15 May 1962 the New York Times reported certain pronouncements by Walter W. Heller on the state of the economy. Speaking of "wistful whispers that a little inflation is good for us," Dr. Heller said: "I claim that anything inflation can do for business and the economy, a good solid expansion can do better — and with healthier long-run results. Price increases may generate optimism, but expansion generates productivity increases. . . ." It is suggested that this association of ideas conveys little meaning, but is another example of how the concept of growth rate can be overworked. One implication here is that under the proper growth-stimulating policies we can achieve full employment without inflation.

The argument in this hypothesis is that under optimal regulation of the aggregate demand the forces of inflation are a function of the level of employment, together with the forces of moral suasion, and that any concepts relating to the rate of growth have no bearing on the matter. Given some particular compromise between inflation and employment, the level of employment cannot be improved — without an increase in the rate of inflation — through special measures aimed at raising the growth rate.

Part IV

On 10 May 1962 Walter P. Reuther stated that union economists place great emphasis on the need for expanding consumer demand through increases in wage rates. This is a view through which the unions have frequently sought public support for their wage demands. It is specious and contrary to the best interests of labor, and should be set to rights for the sake of avoiding the misdirection of public opinion.

Under the controlled state the optimal level of aggregate demand will be maintained independently of how wage rates vary. Wage rates should, of course, be equitable. On the whole the return to labor, as a percentage of the output of the economy, tends to remain close to a fixed value, as observed in Chapter V, and is independent of individual wage bargains. Individual wage bargains should be concerned with relieving local inequities, and should not be concerned with the matter of the purchasing power of the economy.

The argument that increases in wage rates are necessary for the sake of adequate purchasing power has frequently been influential in bringing about inflationary wage pacts. So long as this argument continues to lead to inflationary wage settlements it will interfere with the objective of maintaining a satisfactory level of employment with a tolerable rate of inflation. Thus, while it secures temporary benefits for those receiving the wage rises, it does a disservice for labor as a whole by making the level of employment lower than it would otherwise be.

SECTION 7

AUTOMATION

Part 1

The people of the United States can use all of the goods and services they can possibly produce no matter how much inflation may come along, and with a work week of 40 hours or more. All that is required is that they have the money to buy the things they want. It seems plain that if each person had unlimited funds to buy anything he might wish for, the demand for existing types of goods and services would be staggering compared with our existing capacity to supply, or any capacity that may be anticipated in the foreseeable future. If the people have just the right amount of money, or purchasing power, their demands will be just equal to the capacity to supply. In the controlled economy the government can regulate the purchasing power so that the people will have just enough to absorb the capacity output.

But this is not sufficient to maintain full employment (employment close to 100 percent). One great obstacle will remain. This is inflation.

How this is so is illustrated by the experience of the United States in World War II. During this period almost anyone who wanted a job was able to get one. And the range of opportunities for each person, with regard to type of work and location, was quite wide. With employers ready to receive and train almost any kind of help available the immobility of labor was an almost non-existent problem. But while all of this was fine for labor, on the other side of the coin lay the fact that the inflationary pressures were enormous. Even with price and wage controls inflation proceeded at a rapid pace (largely through quality deterioration); without these controls the rate of inflation would have been far greater than it was.

Under the controlled state, it would be possible for the government to keep conditions in the United States just as they were during World War II, as far as unemployment is concerned. All that is required is to keep the aggregate demand at a suitably high level, and this the government can do. Unemployment would then be at a very low level, and automation would not be looked upon as a scourge, as it sometimes is under less favorable employment conditions. But it is reasonably certain that under this state the rate of inflation would be intolerable. Prices would rise at a rapid rate, and the government would be required to raise the aggregate demand at a correspondingly rapid rate in order to maintain the high level of employment.

So long as this type of behavior is in prospect, the only reasonable course is that of compromise between unemployment and inflation. Under this course it will be more difficult for labor displaced by automation to find new employment. But with the aggregate demand held at the optimum level conditions should be reasonably good in this respect. They will improve as labor and business become more responsive to the forces of moral suasion, permitting of a higher level of employment under the rate of inflation that is tolerated.

But in any case the effects of automation, in displacing labor, will not be cumulative. Some volume of unemployment must exist at any time as a part of the compromise arrangement. There will be a continuous influx, to the ranks of the unemployed, as workers are displaced by automation, and there will be a continuous efflux as workers find new jobs. There is no reason to expect that the percentage of unemployment will increase continuously. It should decrease as society becomes more skilled, or more self-disciplined, in the matter of suppressing the forces of inflation. As society does this it will approach more closely to the employment situation during World War II.

Part II

It is difficult to see what basis there can be for the belief, subscribed to by so many responsible people, that the United States can produce more goods and services than the people can use—or, in other words, that the people cannot use vastly greater quantities of existing types of goods and services than they are now able to purchase. Collateral notions are: (a) that we must find new types of goods and services for the people to spend their money on, (b) that we must reduce the length of the work week, (c) that we must look to foreign markets in disposing of our surplus production, and (d) that expansion of the population will be helpful in offsetting the tendency toward overproduction of existing types of goods and services.

Consider a typical worker in one of the better-paying industries. And let us consider how close he is to the point where he can have all of the things he may want for himself and his family—so much so that a substantial increase in wages will be of little interest to him. How close is he to the point where he does not mind paying taxes, since he does not need any of the things he could buy with these funds? How close is he to the point where he can be quite liberal with his dollars for charity, since he has little need for these funds? How close is he to the point where he would save the bulk of any substantial increase in real income because of being saturated with existing types of goods and services?

The view in this hypothesis is that on all counts he is very far away. In fact, it is held that on no count is there the vaguest suggestion that the gap is closing.

It would seem that there are only a relatively small number of people who stand opposed to the notion that the American people are reaching the saturation point with regard to the use of existing types of goods and services. But even among these it appears that the attitude is generally far more defensive and deferential than would seem appropriate. An utterance on the matter worth noting is one by George Cline Smith of MacKay-Shields Economics, as reported by *U. S. News & World Report,* 18 February 1963: "It's been said that we need a Model-T helicopter in this country to give a new lift to business. Actually, we are far from saturated in more mundane goods. About 11 million families have no automobile. Nine out of ten homes have no air conditioning. Millions of housewives have yet to acquire a clothes dryer."

This type of observation is on the right track, but it is important to note that among the families that do have an automobile and air conditioning and a clothes dryer, and many other conveniences as well, there are relatively few who do not wish for better housing accommodations, more lavish house furnishings, the ability to spend more money on education for their children, the ability to spend more money on entertainment and recreation, and so on. It is a hightly restricted outlook to believe that a family's wants are satisfied when it has one apartment and one washing machine and two automobiles and a fair amount of all the other appliances one can think of.

Prof. Paul McCracken comes closer to the core of the matter when he says (as reported in the same issue of *U. S. News & World Report*): "The idea of a saturation of wants strikes me as unrealistic. The average American income is about $6000 a year. Nearly every family has a long list of products which already exist which they would buy if they had the money. Rising living standards do not make people more satisfied, but only whet their appetite for more."

While there is little sense in the belief that the United States can produce more goods and services than it can use, there is even less sense in the belief that a correction for this fancied fault lies in an expansion of the population. An increase in population brings with it an increased need for goods and services, but it also provides more workers to produce goods and services. There is no reason to believe that the output per man hour of work will diminish as the population increases, as appears to be the hope of those who view the United States as a land of overproduction. Those of us who see the United States as an economy of scarce means, like any other economy since the beginning of civilization, should hope that expansion of the population will not contribute toward reduction of the output per man hour of work.

In his speech of 13 August 1962, President Kennedy, in outlining the favorable prospects facing the nation stated: "And soon that crop of war babies — boys and girls who were born during the war and at the end of the war — will be going to schools and colleges, founding their own homes, buying their own cars and helping to build our prosperity." Here we have the double fallacy — that we tend to overproduce, and that an expansion of the population will help to correct matters — from the President of the

United States, presumably with the approval of his economic advisers. This is a discouraging commentary on the state of development of economic science.

CHAPTER IV

The propensity-to-save-muney, or the PSM, was defined in Section 23 of Chapter II. It is the purpose in this chapter to amplify on the concepts implicit in the definition.

A number of model cases will be presented to illustrate the operation of the PSM in the non-controlled economy. Following this a number of general observations are presented applying to both the non-controlled and controlled economies. These generalizations may be looked upon as a defining hypothesis.

In anticipation of the discussions to follow, it is suggested that the significance of the PSM may best be appreciated when it is recognized that the total muney-savings of the non-controlled economy, which is also the new-muney-rate, is not responsive to the decisions of the people which we ordinarily think of as affecting their muney-savings — namely, decisions relating to spending or the deferment of spending.

It would seem that when the people are disposed toward making heavy expenditures for durable consumer goods and investment, the rate of muney-savings should be relatively low, and that when their inclinations swing in the opposite direction, the rate of muney-savings should rise. But this is not generally so. For, let it be supposed that over some period Ep is constant, and that the new-muney-rate is equal to Ep. This means that the new-muney-rate, or the rate of muney-savings, must be constant. But let it also be supposed that in this period the people have been making heavy expenditures for durable consumer goods and investment, and that they suddenly make a sharp cut in these expenditures. It would seem that this should make the rate of muney-savings rise. But it cannot. So long as Ep remains constant, as assumed, the rate of muney-savings must remain constant, no matter how the people alter their expenditures.

Beyond this it may be observed that when the people make a sharp reduction in expenditures for durable consumer goods and investment, it is usually true that Ep declines, causing the new-muney-rate to decline. Thus, more often than not, a decline in expenditures for durable consumer goods and investment is accompanied by a decline in the rate of muney-savings.

On the other hand, the PSM is a quantity which is responsive to the decisions of the people regarding their expenditures, and in a sense it represents the summation of these decisions. The models illustrate how the relationship between the PSM and the rate of muney-savings influence the behavior of the non-controlled economy.

The model cases to be considered are as follows:

Case I

For this case the conditions in the model economy to be studied are as follows:

*

(1) There are no banking operations. No person either receives or repays a bank loan. Because of this the new-muney-rate is always nil.

(2) Each person's income accrues entirely in the form of cash, whether it be as wages or profit. No part of any income accrues in the form of inventories or receivables.

(3) All expenditures spoken of are purchases of finished goods and services by the ultimate users; and all these purchases are for cash.

(4) In any week the aggregate income of the economy is equal to the aggregate demand, as must be true for any economy. The aggregate income, the aggregate demand, and all components of income and demand spoken of are in monetary measure (current dollars).

(5) As of the time we begin to observe the economy, aggregate income has been constant over the preceding 10 weeks at 1000 units per week. (A unit is some quantity of current dollars.)

(6) When we begin to observe the economy, the spending policies of the people are such that in each week each person spends an amount equal to his average weekly income over the 10 weeks preceding the week in question. The integrated effect of this for the whole economy is that the aggregate demand in any week is 100 percent of the average weekly aggregate income, or aggregate demand, over the preceding 10 weeks.

*

Given these conditions it is a simple matter to see that the aggregate demand must remain constant at 1000 units per week for as long as these conditions continue.

However, let it be supposed that at a given time the spending policies of the people change in this manner:

*

(7) Starting with the given time, each person spends in each week an amount equal to 90 percent of his average weekly income over the preceding 10 weeks. The integrated effect of this for the whole economy is that in each week the aggregate demand is 90 percent of the average weekly aggregate income, or aggregate demand, over the preceding 10 weeks.

*

The first matter of importance is that under the new spending policies the aggregate demand proceeds to fall and continues to do so indefinitely. In the first week after condition (7) goes into effect the aggregate demand is 900 units. In the next week it is 891 units; in the week after that it is 882 units; and so on. After one year the aggregate demand will be in the region of half its original value and will still be in the process of falling.

The rate at which the aggregate demand declines is directly responsive to the spending policies of the people. To see how this is so, let it be supposed that the percentage figure stated in condition (7) rises from 90. As it does so the rate at which the aggregate demand declines slackens off. When this figure reaches 100, the aggregate demand becomes stable, as it was originally. If this figure should rise above 100, the aggregate demand will proceed to rise and will continue to do so as long as the figure in question remains above 100.

On the other hand, the rate of muney-savings of the economy is not responsive to the spending policies of the people. In accordance with condition (1) this rate is always nil. Thus when the people reduce their expenditures in relation to past income — that is, when they reduce the percentage figure in either condition (6) or (7) — this does not lead to an increase in the rate of muney-savings of the economy. But it does give the aggregate demand a downward acceleration, either starting it downward or causing it to decline more rapidly.

It is true that when the people reduce their expenditures in relation to past income, many will increase their individual rates of muney-savings. But there must also be many people whose rates of muney-savings fall, and the summation of the reductions must equal the summation of the increases. It is inescapable that for the whole economy the rate of muney-savings will remain nil so long as Ep is nil and constitutes the whole of the new-muney-rate.

It is a part of the general concept that when the percentage figure in condition (6) or (7) falls, this corresponds to a slackening of the expenditures for durable consumer goods and investment in the actual economy. It is also a part of the general concept that the behavior of the model with this figure less than 100 is analogous to the behavior of the actual economy when it descends into a recession or a depression. Similarly, when this figure is above 100, the behavior of the model is analogous to that of the actual economy when it experiences a boom.

Case II

The economy for this case is generally the same as in Case I, but with these conditions:

*

(8) In each week the banks issue loans in an amount equal to X percent of the average weekly aggregate demand over the preceding 10 weeks, where X is as given below. All loans are to private individuals. Also, for simplicity it is assumed that the banking operations consist entirely of the issue of new loans,

which is to say that no payments are made in discharging existing loans. The rate of new loans, Ep, is the new-muney-rate.

(9) As of the time we begin to observe the economy the aggregate demand has been constant for at least 10 weeks at 1000 units per week.

(10) The spending policies of the people consist of two parts: (a) In each week each person spends an amount equal to 90 percent of his average weekly income over the preceding 10 weeks. (b) In addition, each person receiving a bank loan spends the entire loan in the same week in which it is received.

(11) As of the time we begin to observe the economy X of condition (8) is 10, making the new bank loans in each week 10 percent of recent aggregate demand.

*

Study will show that under these conditions the aggregate demand remains constant at 1000 units per week. In each week the people make purchases of 900 units under condition (10a) and 100 units under condition (10b), making for total purchases of 1000 units.

But it is the object now to observe how the economy behaves when X varies from the value stated in condition (11). For this purpose a sequence of several alterations will be assumed.

For the first alteration it is assumed that X becomes 5. Study will show that under this value the aggregate demand declines continuously after the fashion observed in Case I.

Secondly, given that the aggregate demand has been declining, as a result of the first alteration, and that it is in the region of 800 units per week, let it be supposed that X returns to 10. Study will show that here the aggregate demand soon becomes stable at a value in the region of 800 units per week and remains at that value so long as X remains 10.

Thirdly, proceeding from the last state observed, let it be supposed that X becomes 15. Study shows that here the aggregate demand proceeds to rise and continues to do so as long as X remains 15.

We may now relate the definition of the PSM, as given in Chapter II, to the model. The basic concept attending the PSM is that at any time in the actual economy a particular new-muney-rate will be required to keep the aggregate demand constant. The model illustrates how this may be so. Reviewing the above sequence of changes in X, it may be seen that the aggregate demand will remain constant in the model only when X is 10. This is to say that the aggregate demand will remain constant at any given level only if the new-muney-rate, or Ep, is 10 percent of that level of aggregate demand. This new-muney-rate — 10 percent of aggregate demand — is the PSM for the model under the assumed conditions, in accordance with the definition stated in Chapter II. As is enlarged upon presently, the figure of 10 percent is determined primarily by the spending policies of the people as given by condition (10). It is held that in this type of behavior the model is representative of the actual economy. That is, in the actual economy, as in the model, there will be a particular new-muney-rate required for keeping the aggregate demand constant at any time, and this is determined by the spending decisions of the people.

It may be seen that the PSM in the model is directly responsive to the spending policies of the people. For example, let it be supposed that the percentage figure in condition (10a) changes to 95. Under this assumption X must be 5 in order to keep the aggregate demand constant at any level. This means that the PSM must then be 5 percent of the aggregate demand, as compared with the 10 percent observed previously. Similarly any other change in the percentage figure of condition (10a) will make for a corresponding change in the PSM.

In addition it may be seen that a continuous excess of the PSM over the new-muney-rate causes the aggregate demand to fall continuously, and a continuous excess of the new-muney-rate over the PSM causes the aggregate demand to rise continuously. For example, when X is 5, with matters as stated in condition (10a), the new-muney-rate is 5 percent of current aggregate demand and the PSM is 10 percent, making for an excess of the latter over the former, and the aggregate demand falls.

Study will also show that the rate at which the aggregate demand falls or rises, in the model, is proportional to the amount of the imbalance between the PSM and the new-muney-rate.

Case III

For this case the model is generally the same as in the previous cases, but with these conditions:

*

(12) In each week the banks issue loans to private individuals in the amount of X percent of the average weekly aggregate demand over the preceding 10 weeks, as in Case II.

(13) The government may employ control subsidies to influence the behavior of the aggregate demand. These will be in the form of direct grants to the people, and when they are used the amount in each week is equal to Y percent of the average weekly aggregate demand over the preceding 10 weeks.

(14) As of the time we begin to observe the economy the aggregate demand has been constant for at least 10 weeks at 1000 units per week.

(15) The spending policies of the people consist of these parts: (a) In each week each person spends an amount equal to 90 percent of his average weekly income over the preceding 10 weeks. (b) In addition, each person receiving a bank loan spends the entire loan in the same week in which it is received. (c) In addition, each person receiving a subsidy spends the entire amount in the same week in which it is received.

(16) As of the time we begin to observe the economy the sum of X and Y is 10. The new-muney-rate is the sum of Ep and the rate of control subsidies, and therefore what is assumed here is that the new-muney-rate is 10 percent of recent aggregate demand.

*

Study will show that under these conditions the aggregate demand remains constant at 1000 units per week. If condition (16) is altered so that the sum of X and Y falls below 10, the aggregate demand will fall continuously. Assuming that the aggregate demand has fallen to some level below 1000 units per week — say 900 units per week — and that the sum of X and Y returns to 10, the aggregate demand will soon become stable at a value in the region of 900 units per week. If the sum of X and Y rises above 10, the aggregate demand will rise continuously.

Thus, under the given conditions, there is a PSM in the amount of 10 percent of the aggregate demand. For the aggregate demand can remain constant at any level only if the sum of X and Y is 10, and this means that it can remain constant at any level only if the new-muney-rate is 10 percent of that level. As in Case II the PSM is directly responsive to the spending policies of the people. As the percentage figure in condition (15a) rises or falls, the PSM falls or rises correspondingly.

* * * * *

The PSM of the actual economy is not a measurable quantity with existing techniques. Because of this, and because the concepts attending the PSM involve speculations on the behavior of the actual economy, the definition of the PSM cannot be regarded as a simple statement of fact. Rather, it must be regarded as an hypothesis. The definition given in Chapter II was an abbreviated hypothesis, and it is proposed at this point to present an hypothesis that is more comprehensive. The terms of this are as follows:

*

A. In the simplest view—though one that requires the qualification stated in item B, below—the PSM of the actual economy is a property similar to that observed in the model in Cases II and III. As in those cases it is the new-muney-rate that must be present if the aggregate demand is to remain constant.

In one sense this property is determined by the spending decisions of the people, and represents the integrated effect of these decisions, just as in the model the PSM is determined by the simple spending policies assumed there. But in another sense the PSM is determined by factors of the type that commonly form the basis for short-range business forecasts, since these factors shape or reflect the spending decisions of the people.

The new-muney-rate is determined primarily by the decisions directly relating to the issue of bank credit and has no direct relationship to the spending decisions of the people. When the new-muney-rate is less than the PSM, the aggregate demand declines continuously in a manner that is analogous to the behavior observed in the model cases. When the new-muney-rate is greater than the PSM, the aggregate demand rises continuously.

Given that the aggregate demand is declining, stabilization requires one of two courses or a combination of both. One course is to induce a decrease of the PSM. The non-controlled economy sometimes follows this course, but the methods developed thus far are unreliable. The other course is to raise the new-muney-rate through deficit financing. When this course is followed in the non-controlled economy, it is generally true that a reduction of the PSM occurs as a by-product.

*

B. Let it be supposed that the new-muney-rate is equal to Ep, and that this is constant. Also, let it be supposed that certain stable factors cause the aggregate demand to decline at a steady pace (these factors being of the type that short-range business forecasts are based upon). In addition, let it be supposed that the government is about to intervene for the purpose of stabilizing the aggregate demand, through the use of deficit financing. Assuming that the stable factors referred to remain unchanged, a particular rate of deficit financing will be required, and this will raise the new-muney-rate to a particular level. But this is only partially true. For the manner in which the deficit financing is employed will determine in some measure the amount that is required. This is a difficulty that interferes with a rigorous treatment of the PSM.

It is held, however, that this difficulty is of secondary importance, and that for an approximate analysis it may be neglected. Then, as an approximation, it may be said that the factors causing a steady upward or downward movement of the aggregate demand determine that a particular new-muney-rate is required for a stable (constant) aggregate demand — no matter how it may be provided — and this required new-muney-rate is the PSM. As has been referred to in Section 23 of Chapter II, it is suggested that a similar simplification is implicit in the Keynesian notion that a particular rate of investment is required for any level of aggregate demand.

*

C. As has been indicated, it is a part of the hypothesis that the aggregate demand will rise or fall at a rate that is roughly proportional to the imbalance between the PSM and the new-muney-rate, and that the rate of rise or fall, in percent per year, will be in the region of 3 times the imbalance, when this is in percent of aggregate demand.

*

D. The principal factor determining the PSM in the actual economy is the rate of expenditures for durable consumer goods and investment, the PSM falling as this rate rises. Implicit in this is that an increase in the rate at which merchandise inventories and business receivables accrue makes for a corresponding decrease in the PSM.

*

E. The magnitude of the PSM at any time is determined by two types of factor, namely: (a) the major tangible variables, such as the volume of muney and the level of aggregate demand, and (b) a mass of intangibles which may be summed up as the state of mind of the economy. For practical purposes it may be considered that the tangible variables determine certain limits within which the PSM is free to vary, and that the position of the PSM within these limits is determined by, or reflects, the state of mind prevailing. In general a position of the PSM near the upper limit reflects a highly pessimistic outlook, and a position near the lower limit reflects a highly optimistic outlook.

A factor having a great deal of influence on the limits of the PSM is the ratio of total muney to the aggregate demand, R. As is discussed at length in the work referred to in Chapter I, the limits of the PSM are quite sensitive to changes in R, and because of this the PSM and R have a powerful stabilizing influence on each other. In the United States the value of R has been remarkably stable, at least since the turn of the century, except for intervals attended by great abnormalities. (This is discussed in Chapter VI.) It is speculated that R will be equally stable in the controlled economy. This will be a factor contributing to the stability of the long-term mean of the PSM, as speculated upon in Section 32 of Chapter II.

The PSM in the controlled economy will be determined in the same way as in the non-controlled economy. But because of the greater stability of the state of mind, the limits of the PSM will be much closer together in the controlled economy—making for a much narrower range of variation—for any array of the tangible variables.

*

F. It should always be the object in the controlled economy to keep the aggregate demand rising at some predetermined rate. Because of this the new-muney-rate will have to exceed the PSM by some differential, d, so that the required new-muney-rate will be equal to the quantity (PSM + d). In accordance with the speculations set forth, d, as a percentage of aggregate demand, will have to be in the region of one-third the rate of rise of the aggregate demand, in percent per year. Another speculation, discussed in Chapters II and VI, is that over any moderately long period, such as 10 years, the mean value of the PSM will be in or near the region from 0.5 to 1.1 percent of aggregate demand.

*

G. It is a popular concept that in the course of a depression a decline in purchasing power, due to falling wage rates and employment and profits, contributes to the causes of depression. This view, when employed in an appropriate fashion, may be entirely reasonable. However, in the model cases above the downward movement of the aggregate demand is accounted for entirely in terms of the PSM and the new-muney-rate, without reference to factors such as employment and wage rates. In the same way, any movement of the aggregate demand in the actual economy may be accounted for in terms of the PSM and the new-muney-rate without reference to these other factors. It is true that the factors spoken of havc an influence on the PSM and the new-muney-rate, but given any values of the PSM and the new-muney-rate, these determine the movement of the aggregate demand, and reference to any other factors in accounting for the movement of the aggregate demand is redundant.

*

H. A general principle underlying item D may be stated in this way: The effect of any trend (or situation or development) on the PSM in the non-controlled economy may best be understood by considering the effect it would have on the rate of muney-savings in the controlled economy, the former effect being similar to the latter. For example a decline in investment makes for a component increase in the rate of muney-savings in the controlled economy. It makes for a component increase in the PSM in the non-controlled economy. But it does not make for a component increase in the rate of muney-savings in the non-controlled economy. (The difference lies in the fact that aggregate income remains stable in the controlled economy when investment falls off, but does not do so in the non-controlled economy.)

CHAPTER V

It is the purpose in this chapter to enlarge upon the influence of the planning cushion, as outlined in Chapter II. The analysis here is founded upon certain simple premises. The first is that the only inflationary pressures in the controlled economy will be those which may be described as cost-push, or cost-profit-push, since under proper management there will be no excesses of demand at the existing prices. The aggregate demand will be at the optimal level, and any serious tendencies toward excessive demand in isolated sectors will be suppressed by means of special taxes.

The second premise is that (a) the cost-profit-push pressures will be a function of the level of employment together with whatever moral suasion is brought to bear upon labor and business for restraint in seeking higher wage rates and profit margins, and (b) the monetary and fiscal policies employed in maintaining a given level of employment do not in any way contribute to the inflationary pressures. Or, in other words, for any given percentage of employment, the inflationary pressures cannot be reduced through revision of the monetary and fiscal policies.

A third premise, closely related to the second, is that as the percentage of employment falls, the inflationary pressures generated by labor diminish, and at some low level of employment, such as 93 percent, become nil. As will be seen presently, there is good reason to believe that when the inflationary pressures generated by labor cease, those generated by business cease.

The significance of the planning cushion depends upon several more or less distinct principles. These are outlined separately in the sections following, and are then discussed with regard to their combined effect.

SECTION 1

The *utilization rate* of the economy will be defined as the ratio of the existing rate of output to the capacity rate of output, assuming that there are accepted standards for computing the capacity rate of output. (There may be a considerable amount of disagreement over the matter of defining the capacity output of the economy, but there appears to be general agreement in the matter of estimating the increase in capacity over any period of the order of a year or a few years. While the analysis at this point is in terms of the capacity output, study will show that its validity depends only upon incremental values so that any ambiguity in the capacity output is of little importance.) Study will show that on the basis of this definition and the definition of the planning cushion, the following rule is true: (a) If in any given year the rate of inflation is equal to the planning cushion, the utilization rate will remain constant over that year. (b) If in a given year the rate of inflation exceeds the planning cushion by X percentage points, the utilization rate will decline by X percentage points. For example, given that the utilization rate is 92 percent at the beginning of a given year, that the planning cushion for the year is 1 percent, and that the price index rises by 3 percent over the year, the utilization rate will fall to 90 percent by the end of the year. (c) If in any year the rate of inflation is less than the planning cushion by X percentage points, the utilization rate will rise by X percentage points.

(It should be noted that by the rate of inflation is meant the rate of rise of the price index in percent per year.)

That this rule follows from the definitions may not be immediately obvious, but that it is true may be demonstrated by a simple illustration: Let it be supposed that at the beginning of a given year the aggregate demand is $950,000 per week, but that the capacity output is $1,000,000 per week, both in current dollars, making for a utilization rate of 95 percent. It will also be assumed that for the given year the planning cushion is 1 percent and that capacity rises by 6 percent, in real measure. According to the policy stated in Section 3 of Chapter II, the conditions just assumed require that the aggregate demand be raised in the given year by 7 percent, and at the end of the year it stands at $1,017,000 per week, in current dollars. Now, concerning the rate of inflation, it will be assumed that the price index rises by 3 percent in the given year. Because of this increase in prices, and because of the 6 percent increase in real capacity, the capacity output at the end of the given year is $1,092,000 per week, in current dollars. The utilization rate at the latter time is therefore the ratio of 1,017,000 to 1,092,000, or 93 percent. Thus the utilization rate fell by 2 percent, or the excess of the rate of inflation over the planning cushion, in agreement with the rule.

SECTION 2

There will be a rough correlation between the utilization rate and the percentage of employment. In general a rise (or fall) of the utilization rate will be attended by a rise (or fall) in the percentage of employment, but the change in percentage of employment will generally be only a fraction of the change in utilization rate. Where the change in utilization rate does not exceed 10 percent, the ratio of change in percentage of employment to change in utilization rate may generally be in the region of one-third, and for this analysis it will be taken that one-third is a representative figure. This will not be referred to directly in the discussions to follow, but may serve implicitly as a guide to some of the quantitative relationships involved.

SECTION 3

A factor of some importance is that the return to labor as a whole, expressed as a percentage of the output of the economy, tends to remain constant, or, at least, changes very slowly. One discussion of this matter is presented in *Challenge* of April 1962 under the title *A Law That Cannot Be Repealed.* It is this law which forms the basis for the argument that when the inflationary pressures generated by labor fall to an appropriate level—where in a sense they may be regarded as nil—inflation comes to a halt.

If the law in question is valid study will show that this rule holds true: (a) If the average weekly pay per worker rises at the same rate as the average weekly real output per worker, the price index will remain constant. (b) If the average weekly pay per worker rises faster (or slower) than the average weekly real output per worker, the price index will rise (or fall). (c) If over some moderately long period, such as 5 years, the mean yearly percentage rise in pay per worker exceeds the mean yearly percentage rise in output per worker by X points, the price index will rise at a mean rate close to X percent per year.

This rule would obviously be true if the price of any type of goods were equal to the labor costs involved in producing it. But when this is recognized, it is a simple step from there to recognize that if the average mark-up on goods, above the labor costs, is a fixed percentage of the labor costs, then the rule must be true in the same way as it would be if the price were equal to just the labor costs. That the average mark-up is a fixed percentage of the labor costs is implicit in the law stated at the outset.

It is a basic premise that when the percentage of employment falls, the inflationary pressures generated by labor, in seeking higher wage rates, fall off. When these pressures have subsided to the point where the average rise in pay per worker is equal to the average rise in real output per worker, the inflationary pressures generated by labor may be spoken of as nil. For then, on the average, the labor costs per unit of output remain constant. And at this point the inflationary pressures generated by labor and business combined must be considered nil, for at this point the rise in the price index ceases.

Naturally the law referred to does not operate perfectly, and therefore the rule cannot be regarded as a precise instrument. But it is suggested that the rule may be regarded as a rough approximation to the truth.

SECTION 4

Proceeding from the foregoing observations we may now observe the significance of the planning cushion through certain illustrative cases.

Case I

For the first case let it be supposed that to begin with employment stands at 97 percent of the work force. Secondly, let it be supposed that the legislature adopts a nil planning cushion and that it adheres to this over a long period, such as 10 years or more.

In this case it will be typical for the percentage of employment to fall, and to level off at some relatively low value; and after equilibrium has been reached, the price index will remain constant over the long period. The process by which equilibrium is reached is this: Initially the inflationary pressures are quite high, because of the high level of employment, causing the price index to rise at a fairly rapid rate. So long as the price index rises, with the planning cushion nil, the utilization rate falls, causing the percentage of employment to decline. But as the level of employment falls, the inflationary pressures generated by labor diminish. When employment has reached some low point, such as 94 percent, the inflationary pressures become nil, and thereafter the percentage of employment remains constant, with the price index constant. (This is a simplification, but may be taken as a first approximation to the truth.)

The level of employment at equilibrium will depend in large measure on the degree to which moral suasion has been effective in suppressing the inflationary pressures. Under a relatively weak fabric of moral suasion, as in the United States at the present time, employment may hover in the region of 94 percent. But if the campaign of moral suasion should gather momentum and become a significant factor, the effect will be to raise the equilibrium percentage of employment to a higher level. The process by which the rise occurs will be this: Initially wage rates will rise less rapidly than the average productivity, because of the moral pressures. This will lead to a decline in prices and to an increase in the utilization rate, and therefore a rise in the level of employeemnt. But as employment rises, the inflationary pressures will rise once more, the rise in employment offsetting the effects of moral suasion, and at some point, possibly when employment is in the region of 95 percent, equilibrium will again be established.

It has been suggested that the type of management in this case — maintaining a nil planning cushion — may be regarded as a kind of government neutrality. Under this arrangement the government tolerates no inflation, in the long run; yet it provides a climate in which the people can maintain a satisfactory level of employment if they will maintain suitable self-discipline with regard to the inflationary pressures. Any rise in prices penalizes the people with a fall of the utilization rate and employment. Improvement in the level of employment can be achieved only through an intensification of self-discipline, such as will lead to a fall in prices.

A policy under which the planning cushion is always some positive quantity, leading to continuous inflation, as discussed in the following case, may be regarded by the conservatives as a policy of indulgence. But a policy under which the planning cushion is always negative, leading to a continuous deflation, and a lower level of employment than under a nil planning cushion, cannot serve any useful purpose, and must, even by conservative standards, be considered unjustifiable.

Case II

For the second case, these conditions are assumed: (1) The planning cushion has been nil for a long period of time, and the equilibrium level of employment, with the price index stable, has been 94 percent. (2) There has been widespread dissatisfaction with the high level of unemployment and because of this the legislature now raises the planning cushion to 2 percent. (3) The planning cushion remains at 2 percent indefinitely.

In this case the equilibrium percentage of employment will rise to a higher level, and the economy will settle down to a mean rate of inflation of 2 percent per year over the long period. The process of change is this: Initially the planning cushion is greater than the rate of inflation, which is virtually nil, and the utilization rate rises, leading to a rise in the percentage of employment. As employment rises the inflationary pressures rise, and at some point, possibly when employment stands at 96 percent, the rate of inflation is equal to the planning cushion. Thereafter the level of employment remains constant and the rate of inflation continues at the rate of 2 percent per year. (Again this is a simplification but may be taken as a first approximation to the truth.)

As in the first case, or any similar case that may be assumed, the level of employment at equilibrium will depend upon the state of development of the forces of moral suasion. Under a high state of development of these forces the level of employment at equilibrium will be higher than under a less advanced state. But for any state of development of moral suasion, the level of employment will be higher in this case than when the planning cushion is nil over the long period, or any value less than 2 percent.

SECTION 5

The two cases of Section 4 illustrate the principle that as the planning cushion is raised, the level of unemployment falls and the rate of inflation rises. This means that the level of the planning cushion establishes a compromise between inflation and unemployment. By adjusting the magnitude of the planning cushion the legislature should be able to arrive at a compromise that will be satisfactory to the electorate.

When control is adopted, it is likely that the legislature will have to do a considerable amount of experimenting with the planning cushion. But it would seem desirable that the economy settle down, in time, to a stable planning cushion — stable in the sense that it will remain constant or change slowly. Under a stable planning cushion there will be a stable compromise between inflation and unemployment. There will also be a favorable climate for the forces of moral suasion to bring about continual improvements in the level of employment that may exist under the given planning cushion. And in time the forces of moral suasion may become so effective as to permit of a gradual reduction of the planning cushion and the rate of inflation.

In contrast with this stable type of behavior it is possible that over the long period there will be wide swings of the planning cushion and the rate of inflation. This is to say that there will be alternate periods of indulgence and austerity. Periods of indulgence will be characterized by a relatively high level of employment and a relatively high rate of inflation, attended by widespread dissatisfaction with the rising prices. Periods of austerity will be characterized by a relatively low level of employment and a low rate of inflation, attended by widespread dissatisfaction with the employment situation. Each period will occur as a reaction from the former one, and it will be plain that a stable compromise somewhere between the two extremes would best suit the needs of the people. Competent leadership should be able to bring about a reasonably stable compromise that will meet with the approval of the people.

As to what rate of inflation the economy will tolerate in the interest of minimizing unemployment, only the people can decide. It would seem reasonable to speculate that this may be in or near the region of from 1.5 to 2 percent per year.

It has been said that a stable planning cushion over the long period will provide a favorable climate for the operation of the forces of moral suasion. What is meant, of course, is that the progress of moral suasion under a stable planning cushion will be more rapid than when the planning cushion oscillates between indulgence and austerity over the long period. The campaign of moral suasion will be an effort at developing the self-discipline of the people. It can work best in a disciplined atmosphere. The people must come to feel that a stable compromise between inflation and unemployment will be maintained, and that improvements in employment must come about through their response to the moral suasion effort. They must not be allowed to feel that they will have a way out through a liberalized, or indulgent, planning cushion. They must be led to the realization that such relief will be only temporary— that they will soon tire of the rapid rise in prices— and that only through the development of self-discipline can lasting progress be made.

SECTION 6

It is possible that the campaign of moral suasion will never develop to the point where it will be a significant force in the affairs of the economy. In this case, barring direct price controls or similar restrictive measures, the economy will simply have to rely on the brute force of compromise between inflation and unemployment through choice of the planning cushion. But, on the other hand, when the importance of moral suasion—as a force for approaching full employment with a tolerable rate of inflation—is recognized, the progress in this area may be quite rapid.

Moral suasion must bring with it—as an integral part—the development of standards for judging the merits in disputes over wage rates and pricing policies. It will make little sense to say that a given demand or practice is just or unjust unless there is a reasonable set of standards to judge by. In a sense the development of such standards will represent a gradual and loose approach to price and wage controls. But there will be important differences. First, the standards will not be as rigid as price and wage controls and will give some room for the play of natural forces, including public opinion. Secondly, whatever merits there may be in price and wage controls will be sought out carefully on the basis of experience and the good judgment of the leadership in all segments of the society; whatever evils there may be will be avoided in the same way. For example, it may be that, under the criteria that develop, the profits in a given industry will appear to be too high and that public opinion will be effective in bringing about a reduction in these profits; but it may also be found that the squeeze on profits in this industry has an unfavorable effect on the growth rate and that a revision of the criteria leading to the squeeze is in the best interests of the people. Under gradual and deliberative development of the criteria, unfavorable trends will become apparent, and permit of correction, before a great deal of harm has been done. In contrast, it is likely that the sudden imposition of a rigid system of price and wage controls would do a great deal of harm to many sectors of the economy; moreover, it is likely that even after many years had been spent in efforts to eliminate the inequities introduced, the results would be so discouraging as to lead to abandonment of the price and wage controls.

CHAPTER VI

One purpose in this chapter is to present the basis for the speculations in Section 32 of Chapter II on the probable behavior of the PSM in the controlled economy. This is done in Section 1.

A second purpose is to enlarge on certain observations in Chapter II relating to the policy matters presented in Section 18 of that chapter. This is done in Section 2.

For these discussions reference is made to the experience of the United States from 1902 to the present. For reasons that are discussed at a later point, the periods 1914 through 1922 and 1930 through 1952 are excluded from consideration. It may be noted that the years remaining for consideration were all relatively prosperous ones, except for depressions of minor importance compared to the Great Depression, and were free of wartime anomalies.

SECTION 1

The speculation in Section 24 of Chapter II provides a basis for estimating the mean value of the PSM for each of the years referred to above. The equation involved is

$$Z = 3(S - PSM)$$

where: Z is the percentage rise of the aggregate demand in any given year; S is the increase in the total muney in that year, as a percentage of the volume of aggregate demand in that year; and the PSM is expressed as a percentage of the mean aggregate demand rate for the year.

The table below gives the value of the PSM for each *fiscal* year shown (30 June to 30 June). The aggregate demand was treated as though the value at June 30 of any calendar year was equal to the mean value over that calendar year. Thus Z for any fiscal year is the difference between the mean values of the aggregate demand in the two successive calendar years embracing the given fiscal year. The aggregate demand for the earlier years represented in the table was estimated in the manner indicated in the work referred to in Chapter I.

For many reasons, such as lags in response to changes in the variables, it may be claimed that the PSM as determined in the manner indicated has many ambiguities. It is recognized that from a rigorous standpoint there are certain deficiencies in this treatment. But it is also held that the PSM, as determined in this way, is quite meaningful for the purposes to which the determinations are applied.

Year	PSM	Year	PSM	Year	PSM
1902	1.2	1912	0.4	1953	0.4
1903	0.9	1913	− 1.1	1954	1.8
1904	1.2	1922	1.6	1955	− 0.6
1905	2.7	1923	− 0.4	1956	− 0.3
1906	0.6	1924	1.4	1957	− 0.5
1907	1.2	1925	2.9	1958	2.2
1908	− 0.1	1926	0.1	1959	− 0.4
1909	− 0.5	1927	2.1	1960	− 1.5
1910	1.5	1928	1.9	1961	2.4
1911	2.5	1929	− 1.5	1962	1.3

The grand mean of all the yearly values in the table is 0.8 percent of aggregate demand, and the maximum departure of any yearly value from this mean is 2.3 precentage points. For the period 1902-1913 the mean of all yearly values is 0.9 percent of aggregate demand, and the maximum departure for any year is 2.0 percentage points. For the period 1922-1929 the mean of all values is 1.0 percent of aggregate demand, with a maximum departure of 2.5 percentage points, and for the period 1953-1962 the mean of all values is 0.5 percent of aggregate demand, with a maximum departure of 2.0 percentage points. For any of the three periods the yearly value seldom departed from the mean by more than 1.5 percentage points, and this was true, too, for the departures of the yearly values from the grand mean.

It is held likely that under the controlled state the behavior of the PSM with regard to the mean value over any moderately long period, such as 10 years, will not be very different from what it was over the years represented in the table. This is to say that the mean for any moderately long period will be fairly close to 0.8 percent of aggregate demand, probably not ranging much lower than 0.5 percent of aggregate demand, nor much higher than 1.1 percent of aggregate demand.

It is also held that because of the stable conditions maintained in the controlled economy, the variation of the yearly values of the PSM about the mean for any moderately long period should be much milder than that represented in the table. It would seem reasonable to speculate that the severity of these variations under the controlled state should be of the order of half that represented in the table, or less. The speculation stated in Section 32 of Chapter II allows for a variation somewhat greater than half that over the years considered.

SECTION 2

A quantity of great interest for the years under consideration is the ratio of the total muney to the annual rate of aggregate demand, R. During these years R has always been close to 0.5, and it is held that this has been a systematic characteristic, at least since the turn of the century, for all times other than those in which circumstances were very far removed from normal. It is also held that in the controlled economy R will have a stable characteristic value, and that this will not be greatly different from 0.5.

The periods 1902 through 1913, 1923 through 1929, and 1953 through 1962 are similar in certain basic respects. In each of these periods the average yearly rise of the GNP was between 4 and 5 percent; and in no year did the GNP fall by more than 2 percent. Thus these periods were moderately prosperous and reflect on how R may be expected to behave in prosperous times. In contrast, let us consider the period 1930 through 1932. Here the GNP declined an average of 15 percent a year. Thus, while there were depressions during the periods retained for consideration, these were very mild compared with the Great Depression. During the Great Depression R rose substantially above 0.5 (reaching the value of 0.78 in 1932), but, because of the revolutionary intensity and duration of this depression, it is held that the behavior of R in this period has no sensible relationship to what may be expected in continuously prosperous times. Similarly, during the periods of World Wars I and II there were large excursions of R from 0.5 (extending into the post-war periods) clearly attributable to the wartime anomalies; and therefore these periods are not indicative of the behavior of R under more normal circumstances. However, in the periods that are considered indicative, R has been so remarkably stable that this must be considered to be a systematic characteristic. During these periods R ranged between 0.49 and 0.56 and was rarely greater than 0.54. And since on the whole the economy was moderately prosperous in these periods, it is held likely that R was not greatly different from what it should be under the continuous prosperity of the controlled economy.

Let it be assumed for the moment that it will be characteristic for R to remain close to 0.5 under the controlled state. Then it will also be characteristic that over any moderately long period, such as 5 years, the average new-muney-rate will be close to 0.5 times the average rate of rise of the aggregate demand, where the new-muney-rate is in percent of aggregate demand, and the rate of rise of the aggregate demand is in percent per year. Under the policy stated in Section 18 of Chapter II, Ep is normally restricted to a value which causes the new-muney-rate to be close to 0.5 times the rate of rise of the aggregate demand. Thus the normally restricted value of Ep provides for a new-muney-rate which satisfies the average requirements of the economy.

It is possible, of course, that R will drift away from 0.5 by a significant amount. To observe the effects of such changes in R, let us consider this case: (1) At a given time R is 0.5. (2) Starting with the time in question it becomes characteristic of the economy that in any five-year period the average new-muney-rate required will be 0.4 times the average rate of rise of the aggregate demand. Study will show that because of this characteristic R will drift downward and will settle out at the value of 0.4. (3) The economy follows the policies of Section 18, with the coefficient *c* in equation 1 equal to 0.5.

Study will show that in this case it would be more suitable for the economy to use 0.4 for *c* in equation 1 instead of 0.5 as assumed in condition (3). The question, then, is what is the disadvantage in using the higher value for *c*. This is simply that downward corrections of the aggregate demand, through reduction of Ep below the normally restricted value, will be required more frequently than would be true with the lower value of *c*. The substance of this is that with the lower value of *c* there would be greater stability of Ep. It is to be expected, however, that in a case of this kind the economy would soon detect the desirability of reducing *c* to a more suitable value, and would proceed to do so.

On the other hand, let it be supposed that R rises. Let it be supposed that we have these conditions: (4) At a given time R is 0.5. (5) At the time in question it becomes characteristic of the economy that in any five-year period the average new-muney-rate required will be 0.6 times the average rate of rise of the aggregate demand. This causes R to rise and level off at 0.6. (6) The economy follows the policies of Section 18 with *c* equal to 0.5.

The net effect here is somewhat different from that in the former case. A more suitable value of *c* would be 0.6. Because of condition (6) the normally restricted value of Ep is lower than the average requirement, and this means that upward corrections of the aggregate demand will be required more frequently than would be true with the higher value of *c*. This in turn, means that more control subsidies will be used over the long period. Assuming that it is the object to maintain a balanced budget over the long period, this increased use of control subsidies will lead, instead, toward net deficit financing over the long period. But again it is to be expected that the economy will, in time, perceive this trend and correct for it by raising *c* appropriately.

For an indication of how great the required deficit financing may be in this latter case, let us make these additional assumptions: (7) The economy seeks a balanced budget over the long period, and keeping *c* equal to 0.6 would cause this aim to be realized. (8) The average rate of rise of the aggregate demand over the long period is 6 percent per year.

With *c* held at 0.5, as assumed in condition (6), the normally restricted value of Ep provides a new-muney-rate close to 3 percent of the aggregate demand. With *c* at the more suitable value, or 0.6, the normally restricted value of Ep would provide a new-muney-rate close to 3.6 percent of the aggregate demand. From this it follows that the net deficit financing required over the long period, with *c* held at the less suitable level, will be not more than 0.6 percent of the total volume of aggregate demand in that period (the difference between 3.6 percent and 3 percent).

CHAPTER VII

In this chapter a number of model cases are presented to illustrate the mechanics by which control subsidies and restriction of Ep operate in regulating the aggregate demand. In particular it will be the object to show how control subsidies are effective in offsetting lags in investment.

SECTION 1

In the simple model to be studied there are no taxes; control subsidies are in the form of direct grants to people in the lower income brackets, provided for with funds raised through deficit financing. This will be the equivalent of a reduction of the tax rate on the first income bracket in the actual economy. The model is the same for all of the several cases presented, and has these basic characteristics:

*

(1) The products of the economy may be considered to be divided sharply into two categories. The first of these will be referred to simply as softgoods. These are meant to represent the softgoods and services of the actual economy. The other type of output will be referred to as hardgoods. This component of output represents durable consumer goods, durable producers' goods, and new construction.

(2) The demand for softgoods consists of two components. The primary component in any week will always be equal to 70 percent of the average weekly aggregate demand over the preceeding 20 weeks.

(3) A secondary component of the demand for softgoods will appear as a result of control subsidies. In any week this component of demand will be equal to the average weekly issue of control subsidies over the preceding 20 weeks.

(4) The demand for hardgoods consists of two components. The primary component in any week will be equal to X percent of the average weekly aggregate demand over the preceding 60 weeks. At this point it may be said that a typical range of X will be between 24 and 30, but this will be dealt with more specifically in the cases following. Assuming that at some time X is 27, we may say, for ease of expression, that the primary demand for hardgoods is 27 percent of past aggregate demand.

(5) The secondary component of demand for hardgoods is provided through Ep. In any week this component will be equal to the average weekly value of Ep over the preceding 30 weeks.

(6) The desired curve of aggregate demand always rises at the rate of 6 percent per year.

Case I

The purpose in this case is to show some aspects of how control subsidies serve to compensate for lags in the demand for hardgoods (or investment). For this case these conditions are assumed:

*

(7) In any week Ep will always be 3 percent of the aggregate demand in that week.

(8) The primary demand for hardgoods is 29 percent of past aggregate demand and will remain at this value until altered by subsequent assumptions.

(9) No control subsidies are currently in use. This will continue until altered by subsequent assumptions.

*

One way of studying a case of this kind is to start with an assumed table of numbers representing values of the several factors over 60 consecutive weeks, and proceed to observe developments from these values in accordance with the assumed behavior characteristics. When this method, or some equivalent, is used, and when the numbers assumed are reasonable, it is found that the economy approaches a steady-state condition over a fairly short period of time. Conditions will ordinarily be close to steady-state after a few months from the start of the observations.

When the steady-state has been reached in this case, it is found that these conditions exist: (a) The aggregate demand rises at a rate near 6 percent per year, the desired rate of rise. (b) In any week the demand for softgoods is approximately 69 percent of the aggregate demand in that week, and the demand for hardgoods is the remainder, or 31 percent of current aggregate demand.

For future reference it will be assumed that when the steady-state has been reached, the aggregate demand is at a satisfactory level and is aligned in a satisfactory manner with respect to capacities in the softgoods and hardgoods sectors.

Let it be supposed, now, that at a given time the primary demand for hardgoods changes. Specifically, let it be supposed that:

*

(10) At the given time the primary demand for hardgoods becomes 27 percent of past aggregate demand.

*

Here study will show that when the steady-state has been reached, the aggregate demand is very close to static. That is, the rate of rise is essentially nil. This is an unsatisfactory state, considering that the desired curve of aggregate demand is rising at the rate of 6 percent per year. Control subsidies will serve as a remedy, and it is assumed that:

*

(11) Control subsidies at the rate of 2 percent of the aggregate demand are introduced.

*

Study shows that after the steady-state has been arrived at, these conditions exist: (a) The aggregate demand rises at the rate of 6 percent per year. (b) The current demand for softgoods is approximately 71 percent of the current aggregate demand, with the demand for hardgoods 29 percent of the aggregate demand.

Noteworthy indications of this case, which may be regarded as basic principles, are these:

*

A. For the sake of keeping the aggregate demand at the proper rate of rise, the proper rate of control subsidies will compensate for any lag in the demand for hardgoods. But, as is discussed in item C, below, there is a question as to whether or not this will be adequate in all cases.

*

B. If the rate of control subsidies in condition (11) had been made larger than 2 percent of the aggregate demand, the rate of rise of the aggregate demand would have been correspondingly greater. This means that if a rapid upward correction of the aggregate demand is required, it can be readily accomplished through a suitably high rate of control subsidies.

*

C. An important feature of this case is the shift in the proportions of the demands for hardgoods and softgoods after the introduction of conditions (10) and (11). Originally the current demand for hardgoods was 31 percent of the current aggregate demand. But under the new conditions this becomes 29 percent of the aggregate demand. An implication of this is that the control scheme is satisfactory only so long as the change in the primary demand for hardgoods is relatively small. If there should be a large and sudden fall in the primary demand for hardgoods, serious defects in the control scheme would be manifest. It is a part of the hypothesis that disruptive changes of this kind are not to be expected in the controlled economy. This is discussed in Section 2. Before proceeding to this discussion, however, it is desirable that the difficulties involved be illustrated. This is done in Case II.

Case II

This case deals with the effects of a large and sudden drop in the primary demand for hardgoods. Here the following conditions are assumed:

*

(12) To begin with the economy is in the same steady-state as at the beginning of Case I, the primary demand for hardgoods being 29 percent of past aggregate demand.

(13) To begin with the employment situation is generally satisfactory; the demand for hardgoods is near the capacity level, and the demand for softgoods is near the capacity level.

(14) At a given time the primary demand for hardgoods falls to 19 percent of past aggregate demand and remains at this value indefinitely.

(15) About 2 months after the drop in the primary demand for hardgoods, the government introduces control subsidies at the rate of 10 percent of the aggregate demand, and these continue indefinitely.

*

Study will show that after the steady-state has been reached, the following conditions exist: (a) The aggregate demand is rising at a rate close to 6 percent per year. (b) The aggregate demand is roughly 10 percent below the desired curve. (c) The demand for softgoods is near the capacity of the softgoods sectors. (d) The demand for hardgoods is close to two-thirds the capacity of the hardgoods sectors.

The question here is that of what action the government should take. It would be a simple matter for the government to drive the aggregate demand up to the original desired curve, but it is not likely that this would be a satisfactory procedure. It is almost certain that it would produce excessive inflationary pressures in the softgoods sectors without making for a significant improvement in employment in the hardgoods sectors. Thus it appears that the economy would have to be content to employ control subsidies in a manner that would keep the demand for softgoods at a satisfactory level and explore methods other than those embraced by the proposed control scheme for correcting the demand in the hardgoods sectors.

It is held, however, that extreme depression of the demand for hardgoods, such as that assumed in this case, is not to be expected so long as the demand for softgoods is kept at a satisfactory level. This is discussed in the following section.

SECTION 2

In examining the question of instability of the demand for hardgoods, we may begin by considering the reason for instability in the non-controlled economy.

Let us return to Case I, above, with the primary demand for hardgoods at 29 percent of past aggregate demand, so that the aggregate demand rises at the desired rate and conditions are generally satisfactory. Then, let it be supposed that the primary demand for hardgoods falls to 27 percent of past aggregate demand. As was observed previously, the rise of the aggregate demand ceases, so that the aggregate demand becomes static.

Given this state of affairs in the non-controlled economy, conditions are conducive to a further decline in the demand for hardgoods; for there will be predictions of a recession or depression, with a general decline of optimism. Let it be supposed, therefore, that the primary demand for hardgoods falls to 25 percent of past aggregate demand. Now the aggregate demand proceeds to fall at a rate near 6 percent per year. This contributes toward a further decline in the demand for hardgoods, accelerating the rate of fall of the aggregate demand, and the vicious cycle is on.

Thus in the non-controlled economy a small decline in the expenditures for hardgoods sets in motion a train which may lead to a very large decline in these expenditures. But in the controlled economy the early use of control subsidies prevents the vicious process from getting started. It is held, therefore, that the instabilities of the demand for hardgoods in the non-controlled economy are not to be taken as an index of the performance of the controlled economy.

For a closer view of the matter we may refer to the experience of the United States over the past 10 years. This is a period during which the economy was moderately prosperous, without significant anomalies, and for which reliable statistics are available. The quantities of interest for this period are: (a) total expenditures for durable consumer goods, producers' durable equipment, and new construction, and (b) the GNP minus all government purchases of goods and services, or the private aggregate demand. The ratio of quantity (a) to quantity (b) for each of the years from 1952 through 1961, in percent, is as follows:

1952	27.9 %	1957	29.4 %
1953	29.3 %	1958	27.6 %
1954	28.6 %	1959	28.6 %
1955	30.4 %	1960	27.8 %
1956	29.7 %	1961	26.6 %

The mean value of the quantities shown is 28.6 percent, and it may be seen that the maximun departure from the mean for any year was 2.0 percent of the aggregate demand.

It is held that this data demonstrates a characteristic stability of the demand for hardgoods, in relation to the private aggregate demand, in moderately prosperous times. Beyond this, it is held that under the controlled state the stability will be even greater. It is suggested as probable that over any moderately long period, such as 10 years, the demand for hardgoods in any year will rarely depart from the mean in that period by more than 1 percent of the private aggregate demand.

Some people may hold that this outlook is specious. They may hold that purchases of softgoods and services tend to rise and fall proportionately with changes in expenditures for hardgoods, but that the rate of purchase of hardgoods is the prime mover; if the government causes the purchases of softgoods and services to follow a stable course, this will not necessarily cause the prime mover to follow a commensurate course.

The concept here is that under the controlled state the demand for softgoods and services will lead the way, as the prime mover, and that the demand for hardgoods will follow. The people who derive their income from the softgoods and services sectors will provide a stable component of demand for durable consumer goods and residential construction. In addition, because of the favorable prospects for investment in these sectors, there will be a stable component of demand for producers' durable equipment and industrial construction in these sectors. These components of demand will provide the backbone for a stable over-all demand for hardgoods.

The principle involved may be illustrated by this simple analogy: Let it be supposed that income in the softgoods and services sectors is always 1000 units per year, and that the people in these sectors always spend 30 percent of their income for hardgoods. Also, let it be supposed that they purchase these goods from a particular segment of the economy, segment A. These purchases thus provide segment A with a stable income of 300 units per year. Then, let it be supposed that the people of segment A always spend 30 percent of their income for hardgoods, and that they purchase these from segment B. Similarly, the people of segment B spend 30 percent of their income for hardgoods and purchase these from segment C. And so on. This leads to a series whose sum is 429 units per year, and this is a constant demand for hardgoods, for the whole economy, resulting from the demand for hardgoods provided by the people associated with the softgoods and services sectors.

It is held that this illustration is analogous to the way in which a stable over-all demand for hardgoods will obtain in the actual controlled economy as a result of the stable conditions maintained in the softgoods and services sectors. It is suggested, too, that the performance of the United States in the past 10 years reflects this type of behavior. It is held that this performance is an index of what may be expected under the controlled state, and that even greater stability of the demand for hardgoods is to be expected because of the greatly reduced influence of disruptive psychological factors.

From these observations it may seem that it would be preferable for the government to concentrate on regulating the demand for softgoods and services instead of concentrating on regulation of the aggregate demand in the manner proposed. This alternate course would be worthy of study, and might constitute a worthwhile refinement. But it is held likely that any advantages that might result would not be sufficiently great to warrant the greater complexities involved in planning and execution.

SECTION 3

Assuming that the demand for hardgoods will remain a stable proportion of the aggregate demand under the controlled state, a major question remains. Let it be supposed that to begin with (just after control has been adopted) there is an excessive amount of capacity in the hardgoods sectors, making for a large component of unemployment in these sectors. The question here is that of how the economy should proceed in correcting matters.

One course is to depend upon what may be regarded as a normal adjustment. Conditions will be favorable for a transfer of labor from the hardgoods sectors to the other sectors. Conditions will become more favorable as the demand for softgoods and services is pressed to a higher level, and the limitations on this will be only the inflationary pressures that are generated. The processes in this adjustment will be no different from those which must occur when automation displaces a large number of workers in any sector of the economy, or when there is a natural shift of demand from certain sectors of the economy to others.

The second course is that of providing an artificial stimulus to the demand for hardgoods, as through subsidies on investment. The justification for this course will be the promotion of an accelerated growth rate or the relief of regional hardships. Where the object is an accelerated growth rate, the artificial stimulus should be continued as long as it is deemed worthwhile. Where the object is the relief of regional hardship, management should aim at the transfer of labor from the sectors requiring artificial stimulus in order that the stimulants may be discontinued, thus bringing about a natural alignment between the demand and the supply capabilities.

If the United States were to adopt control at this time, raising the aggregate demand to the optimal level, excessive capacity in the hardgoods sectors would be revealed if a preponderant part of the unemployment then existing was in these sectors. It is suggested that there are no reliable indications that this would be so. It is certainly improper to arrive at any such estimate on the basis of the performance of the economy during lags in activity, as in the past few years.

SECTION 4

Three additional cases are presented in this section to illustrate the mechanics of control.

Case III

This case deals with the prevention of excessive aggregate demand through reduction of Ep. To begin with the economy is in the same steady-state as at the beginning of Case I; the primary demand for hardgoods is 29 percent of past aggregate demand, and the aggregate demand is rising at the rate of 6 percent per year. Also, the aggregate demand is on the desired curve.

Let it be supposed, now, that the primary demand for hardgoods rises to 31 percent of past aggregate demand. The aggregate demand suffers an immediate rise of 2 percent, and thereafter rises at close to 12 percent per year.

However, shortly after the accelerated rise has been observed, Ep is reduced to 1 percent of aggregate demand. Soon after this a steady-state is reached in which the aggregate demand rises at the desired rate of 6 percent per year; but the aggregate demand lies somewhat above the desired curve, rising parallel with it. If Ep is reduced to zero, the aggregate demand will fall to the desired curve; and if Ep is then restored to 1 percent of aggregate demand, the aggregate demand will remain on the desired curve (with slight deviations while steady-state conditions are being reached). In the steady-state the demands for hardgoods and softgoods will have the same proportions as they did originally.

Case IV

This case deals with the possibility that reduction of Ep will sometimes be inadequate in preventing excessive demand although it is held that this will be true only under circumstances which will be so unusual that they may properly be regarded as revolutionary.

Let it be supposed that in a case similar to Case III the primary demand for hardgoods rises to 34 percent of past aggregate demand. Here reduction of Ep to zero can only partially compensate for the disturbance. The remedy will lie in a special tax program, such as emergency taxes or special stand-by taxes.

Any form of taxes will do, but it would be preferable to apply the taxes so that they directly detract from the excesses of demand, as would sales taxes applied to the goods most affected by the excesses. It has been observed that control subsidies are effective in compensating for lags in the demand for hardgoods. In the same way any program of taxes will be effective in compensating for excesses of demand for hardgoods.

Case V

This case deals with the possibility that changes in the demand for softgoods will disturb the course of the aggregate demand. This is to assume that the primary demand for softgoods, as given in condition (2) may vary.

Let it be supposed that this component of demand falls to 68 percent of past aggregate demand. It is plain that this can readily be compensated for with control subsidies in the amount of 2 percent of aggregate demand.

However, let it be supposed that this quantity rises to 72 percent of past aggregate demand. It is less obvious that this development can be compensated for by a reduction of Ep in the amount of 2 percent of aggregate demand. But study will show that this is true in the same way that control subsidies serve to compensate for a lag in the demand for hardgoods.

SECTION 5

The observations in this section are of some importance in connection with the discussions in Chapter VIII, relating to the matter of how rapidly the aggregate demand will respond to the control devices, or, more generally, how well the government can keep the aggregate demand in the vicinity of the desired curve.

Given that the model economy is as defined by conditions (1) through (5), study will show that the PSM is a function of the primary demand for hardgoods in the sense that the PSM will change only with changes in this component of demand. Study will show that when the primary demand for hardgoods is 30 percent of past aggregate demand, the PSM is zero; when the former figure is 29 percent, the PSM is 1 percent of aggregate demand; when the former figure is 28 percent, the PSM is 2 percent of aggregate demand; and so on. (This is discussed at greater length in Chapter VIII.) It is not implied by this that the PSM of the actual economy is determined entirely by the demand for hardgoods, but it is held that this is largely true, and it simplifies matters to construct the model so that the PSM does change only with the demand for hardgoods.

Proceeding from these observations it may be seen that the model is constructed so as to be consistent with the speculation stated in Section 24 of Chapter II, regarding the rate of rise of the aggregate demand as a function of the relationship between the PSM and the new-muney-rate. Given that the new-muney-rate in the model (this is the sum of Ep and the control subsidies) exceeds the PSM by X percent of the aggregate demand, the aggregate demand will rise at a rate close to 3X percent of itself per year. This will be found true for any values that are assumed in the model for Ep, the primary demand for hardgoods, and the rate of control subsidies.

It is suggested that because the model behaves in this way, it can be useful in estimating the behavior of the actual economy in response to manipulations of the control devices. The model is used in this way in the studies of Chapter VIII.

CHAPTER VIII

One purpose in this chapter is to present certain rational considerations supporting the belief that the control policy, as outlined in Section 18 of Chapter II, will be suitable for the economy and will lead close to a balanced budget over the long period, assuming that this is the objective and that the economy is capable of operating in what has been referred to as the probable mode. This is done in Section 1.

A second purpose is to present rational considerations supporting the speculations in Section 35 of Chapter II on how closely the economy can hold the aggregate demand to the desired curve. This is done in Section 2.

SECTION 1

The analyses concerning the effects of control policy on the budget over the long period are made in connection with a model economy that is essentially the same as that in Chapter VII but with certain additional conditions. The characteristics of the model are these:

*

(1) The economy maintains a tax program that yields revenues in the amount of 0.5 percent of the aggregate demand. When control subsidies are not used the taxes make for a budgetary surplus of 0.5 percent of the aggregate demand. When control subsidies are used they will ordinarily be used at a rate greater than 0.5 percent of aggregate demand, and then there will be a budgetary deficit equal to the difference between the control subsidies and the taxes.

(2) At all times in which downward corrections of the aggregate demand are not required, Ep will be restricted to (0.5 + 0.5Z) percent of the aggregate demand, where Z is the yearly percentage rise of the desired aggregate demand curve at the time in question.

It is a part of the general hypothesis that the demand for Ep will almost always be sufficiently brisk, under suitable management of the interest rate, to keep Ep up to the restricted value. The discussions will proceed on the assumption that Ep is always at the restricted value. The effects of departures of Ep from the restricted value are discussed at a later point.

(3) For simplicity it will be assumed that the rate of rise of the desired aggregate demand curve is always 6 percent per year. What is said for the operation of the economy under this assumption will be substantially true for any other rate of rise within reasonable limits. Under this assumption, and under the assumption in item (2), Ep will always be restricted to 3.5 percent of the aggregate demand, except when downward corrections of the aggregate demand are required.

(4) When upward corrections of the aggregate demand are required, these will be accomplished through the use of control subsidies. At these times, according to the above assumptions, Ep will be 3.5 percent of the aggregate demand.

(5) When downward corrections of the aggregate demand are required, these will be accomplished through reduction of Ep to a value below 3.5 percent of the aggregate demand. At these times control subsidies will be nil. (According to earlier assumptions, control subsidies must continue for at least 3 months after they have been introduced. Therefore it is more correct to say that if control subsidies are not nil when the need for downward correction of the aggregate demand appears, they will be discontinued at the earliest possible time.)

(6) It will be assumed that the PSM has a mean value over the long period of 1 percent of the aggregate demand, and that it may range between zero and 2 percent of the aggregate demand. This is reasonably consistent with the speculation in Section 32 of Chapter II. Effects of excursions beyond these assumed limits will be considered in the discussions.

(7) The primary demand for softgoods will always be 70 percent of past aggregate demand, as stated more specifically in item (2) of Chapter VII. The secondary demand for softgoods will be equal to

the past average issue of control subsidies, as stated in item (3) of Chapter VII.

(8) The primary demand for hardgoods will be a percentage of past aggregate demand, as stated in item (4) of Chapted VII. As is brought out in the discussions below, the assumption in item (6) concerning the PSM determines that this percentage will have a mean value of 28.5 and may range between 27.5 and 29.5.

(9) The secondary demand for hardgoods will always be equal to the past average value of Ep, as stated in item (5) of Chapter VII.

*

It was observed in the latter part of Chapter VII that there is a relationship between the PSM and the primary demand for hardgoods. The relationship is slightly different for this model from that observed in Chapter VII, because of the element of taxes, and it is necessary to establish what this is. For this purpose let it be supposed that these conditions exist: (a) Ep is nil, (b) there are no control subsidies, and (c) the primary demand for hardgoods is 30 percent of past aggregate demand. In this case, after the steady-state has been reached the aggregate demand will be constant; and therefore the PSM is equal to the existing new-muney-rate. With control subsidies nil there is a budgetary surplus of 0.5 percent of aggregate demand, and with Ep nil this makes new-muney-rate equal to minus 0.5 percent of the aggregate demand. This is the PSM under the assumed conditions.

But study will show that the PSM is determined only by condition (c), the primary demand for hardgoods. For if Ep and the control subsidies are allowed to vary from zero, while condition (c) remains unchanged, their algebraic sum must always be zero if the aggregate demand is to remain constant. Therefore the PSM must always be minus 0.5 percent of aggregate demand so long as the primary demand for hardgoods is 30 percent of past aggregate demand.

In the same way it is found that: when the primary demand for hardgoods is 29.5 percent of past aggregate demand, the PSM is zero; when the former figure is 28.5 percent, the latter figure is 1 percent of aggregate demand; when the former figure is 27.5 percent, the latter is 2 percent; and so on.

The discussions at this point will be facilitated by considering at the outset two steady-state conditions. In the first of these the PSM is 2 percent of aggregate demand, Ep is 3.5 percent of aggregate demand, and control subsidies are employed at the rate of 1 percent of aggregate demand. Study will show that in the steady-state the aggregate demand rises at the rate of 6 percent per year, which by the assumptions is the desired rate. There is a budgetary deficit at the rate of 0.5 percent of aggregate demand.

In the second steady-state condition the PSM is zero, Ep is 2.5 percent of aggregate demand, and there are no control subsidies. Here too the aggregate demand rises at the rate of 6 percent per year. There is a budgetary surplus at the rate of 0.5 percent of aggregate demand.

Proceeding from these steady-state conditions, it is the object now to consider three cases in which the PSM varies in some regular pattern. For the first case it is assumed that the PSM varies in this way: For one full year the PSM is 2 percent of aggregate demand, in the following year it is zero, in the next year it returns to the higher value, in the next year it is zero, and so on. It may be noted that in this case the behavior of the PSM satisfies the assumed condition that the mean value over the long period will be 1 percent of aggregate demand. The variation of the PSM in this way will require appropriate manipulation of the control devices, and for the control procedure this highly unrealistic assumption is made: The government knows at all times how the PSM is varying and manipulates the controls in accordance with this knowledge; when the PSM rises to the upper value, control subsidies at the rate of 1 percent of aggregate demand are introduced and Ep is restricted to 3.5 percent of aggregate demand; when the PSM falls to the lower value, the control subsidies are discontinued, and Ep is restricted to 2.5 percent of aggregate demand.

The observations above on the steady-state conditions are useful in understanding the performance of the aggregate demand in this case, since the economy comes close to alternating between the two steady-states. These observations suggest that the aggregate demand will follow the desired curve, assuming that it was on the desired curve to begin with. This is not strictly true because of the transient effects each time the PSM changes. But it is substantially true; the aggregate demand will follow the desired curve with relatively small oscillations about it. Considering, now, the behavior of the budget, the assumed control procedure determines that there will be alternate years of surplus and deficit in the amount of 0.5 percent of the aggregate demand. Thus, over the long period the budget is balanced.

When a more realistic procedure for manipulating the controls is considered, as in Section 2, the behavior of the budget is substantially the same as under the procedure here.

For the second case, let it be supposed that the PSM varies in a manner similar to that just considered, but that the upper and lower values are 1.5 and 0.5 percent of the aggregate demand. It may be noted that here again the behavior satisfies the condition that the mean value over the long period be 1 percent of aggregate demand. In addition it will be assumed that the control procedure is similar to that in the first case, Ep and the control subsidies being adjusted by the amounts necessary to keep the aggregate demand substantially on the desired curve. In this case the budget will alternate yearly between a balanced status and a surplus in the amount of 0.5 percent of aggregate demand. Over the long period there will be a net budgetary surplus having a mean yearly value of 0.25 percent of aggregate demand.

For the third case it will be assumed that the variation of the PSM is similar to that in the first two cases; but for the moment condition (6) will be set aside, and it will be assumed that the upper and lower values of the PSM are 3 and minus 1 percent of the aggregate demand. Here the budget will alternate yearly between a surplus of 0.5 percent of aggregate demand and a deficit of 1.5 percent of aggregate demand. Over the long period there will be a net deficit having a mean yearly value of 0.5 percent of aggregate demand. Thus, even though the PSM swings much more widely than is believed to be representative for the actual controlled economy, the adverse effects on the budget over the long period are rather insignificant.

* * * * *

It is held that these cases are representative of how the United States would behave under the control policy embodied in equation 2 of Section 18, Chapter II, with possible modifications on the basis of experience. Over any moderately long period, such as 5 years, there might be a net budgetary surplus or deficit having an average value somewhere between zero and 0.5 percent of aggregate demand, depending upon the behavior of the PSM and the adjustments in policy. It is likely, however, that the net budgetary surplus over any moderately long period will seldom have an average value greater than 0.25 percent of aggregate demand, as in the second case above. It is also likely that the net budgetary deficit over any moderately long period will seldom have an average value greater than 0.25 percent of aggregate demand, and that for practical purposes a value of 0.5 percent, as in the third case, may be taken as a limiting value.

The proposed control policy is founded on the premise that the demand for Ep will always cause Ep to be equal to the restricted value. Occasional lags in the demand may be tolerated without strenuous efforts for correction through reduction of the interest rate. These, of course, may have to be compensated for with control subsidies. Large and frequent lags will require more strenuous efforts at correction through reduction of the interest rate, and possibly through other means, such as subsidies on investment. But if the lags persist, or if large quantities of subsidies on investment are required to overcome them, it is likely that the economy will not be able to maintain a balanced budget under any control policy, and the proposed policy will be meaningless. If this should be so, the economy will have to follow a policy along the lines suggested in Section 38 of Chapter II.

SECTION 2

The object in this section is to present certain rational considerations underlying the speculation in Section 35 of Chapter II, relating to the matter of how closely the economy can hold the actual demand to the desired curve. In the previous section it was assumed that the PSM varied in a regular pattern, and an unrealistic control procedure was assumed for dealing with this behavior. In this section we shall again assume a regular pattern of variation for the PSM, but here a more realistic control procedure will be assumed, and the response of the aggregate demand will be examined.

The control procedure to be employed here consists of certain rudimentary rules. These are assumed only for purposes of study in relation to the model case to be considered. It is not implied that these rules should be eminently suitable in the program of control for the actual economy. In the actual economy it should be a simple matter for the executive department to formulate similar, more sophisticated rules for its own guidance and refine these through experience. But in addition, an important element

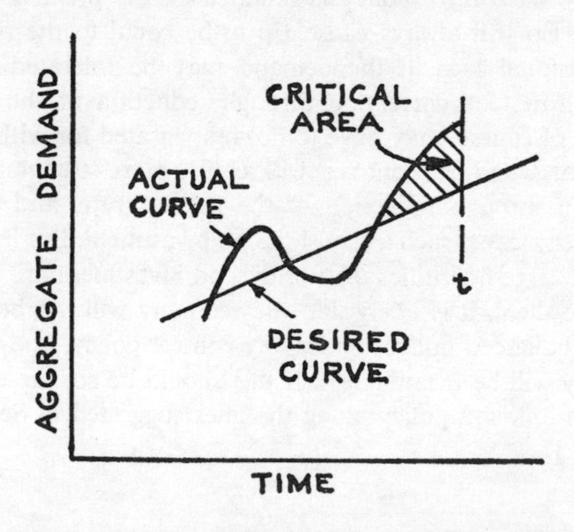

FIGURE 1

of control in the actual economy will be the ability of the control authority to anticipate the need for control actions, on the basis of economic indicators, and to estimate the most appropriate magnitude of control application in any situation.

The model economy is the same in all respects as that in Section 1, and it is implicit in the discussions that Ep is always at the restricted value. If Ep should generally lag behind the restricted value, this will not materially affect the accuracy with which the actual demand can be held to the desired curve. This is discussed at a later point.

The rules that will govern the application of the controls in the model are these:

*

Rule 1: This rule deals with the matter of *when* corrective action shall be taken. The actual curve of aggregate demand will be comprised of a series of oscillations about the desired curve, as in Figure 1. At any given time, t, the area between the two curves from the time of the last intersection, referred to as the critical area, will be the criterion governing the initiation of corrective action. The critical area represents a volume of aggregate demand (rate of aggregate demand multiplied by time). Corrective action will be taken when this area is equal to 0.5 percent of the current yearly aggregate demand.

*

Rule 2: (a) When an upward correction of the aggregate demand is required (critical area below the desired curve) control subsidies will be introduced at the rate of 2 percent of the aggregate demand. According to the assumptions on general control policy, these must continue for at least 3 months. If at the end of this time the aggregate demand rate has not risen to the point where it touches the desired curve, the subsidies will be continued until the aggregate demand has done so, and at this point the subsidies will be discontinued. (b) When a downward correction of the aggregate demand is required, Ep will be reduced from its normal value by 2.5 percent of the aggregate demand. According to the assumptions in Section 1, this means that when a downward correction is required, Ep will be reduced to 1 percent of the aggregate demand. This reduction of Ep will be continued until the aggregate demand has fallen to the point where it touches the desired curve, after which

Ep will be restored to its normal value, or 3.5 percent of aggregate demand.

*

To observe the manner in which the economy responds to the controls, this case will be assumed: As of the beginning of a given calendar year the aggregate demand has been following the desired curve for more than 1 year, with the PSM at its mean value of 1 percent of aggregate demand. At the time in question the PSM falls suddenly to nil and remains at this value for 1 year. At the end of this time the PSM rises suddenly to 2 percent of aggregate demand and remains at this value for 1 year. At the end of this time the PSM again falls to nil, continuing at this value for 1 year; and this yearly alternation of the PSM between the values of zero and 2 percent of aggregate demand continues indefinitely.

What happens to the aggregate demand in this case is clearly determined by the assumed conditions. A summary of the behavior is this: The rate of aggregate demand follows an irregular pattern, but at no time does this rate depart from the desired curve by more than 3 percent. For any calendar year the volume of aggregate demand never departs from the desired volume by more than 1.5 percent, and seldom is this departure more than 1.2 percent.

* * * * *

This and similar studies form the basis for the speculations in Section 35 of Chapter II. How much support is given to these speculations by studies of this kind is a matter of intuition.

As was observed at the end of Chapter VII, the model is constructed so that it conforms to the speculation in Section 24 of Chapter II. The principal assumptions, or speculations, determining this behavior are the 20 weeks averaging period in conditions (2) and (3) of Chapter VII, the 30 weeks averaging period in condition (5) of Chapter VII, and the 60 weeks averaging period in condition (4) of Chapter VII. These factors also determine the lags in the model in response to the controls. It is held that the correspondence between the model and the actual economy with regard to the behavior dealt with in Section 24 of Chapter II imparts a large measure of validity to the model in representing the lags in response to be expected in the actual economy.

One of the more important factors to be weighed is the response of the aggregate demand to reductions of Ep. It is entirely possible that in the actual economy the response will be considerably more sluggish than that provided by the terms of the model, particularly condition (5) of Chapter VII. But when it is considered that reduction of Ep should have a fast-acting effect on such things as new housing starts and installment purchases, it is not unreasonable to expect that the response of the actual economy may be comparable to that of the model.

A factor contributing heavily toward superior performance of the actual economy, over that of the model, will be discretionary application of the controls, guided by the economic indicators. Even if the response of the actual economy to reductions of Ep should prove to be more sluggish than in the model, it is likely that this will be largely offset, in general, by the ability of the control authority to anticipate the need for reducing Ep at an earlier time than would be indicated by the simple rules of the model, together with the ability to estimate the most appropriate magnitude of change in Ep.

What has been said for the response to reductions in Ep applies equally well to the response to control subsidies. Review of condition (3) of Chapter VII suggests that the response of the actual economy is likely to be better than that of the model. But in any case, discretionary application of the control subsidies should contribute heavily toward better performance of the actual economy over that of the model.

Another factor is the matter of how the PSM may be expected to vary. It is a part of the general hypothesis that the variation assumed in the model case is more severe than would be representative of the actual economy. It is held that for any year the mean value of the PSM will generally differ from the long-term mean by much less than the 1 percent of aggregate demand assumed for each year in the model case. In addition it is to be expected that in the actual economy the PSM will generally change gradually, rather than stepwise from one extreme to the other, as in the model. This will be of importance in predicting the future behavior of the aggregate demand, at any time, for the sake of anticipating the need for control actions.

A premise for these discussions has been that the demand for Ep will always be sufficient to keep Ep at the restricted value. If this premise should prove to be untrue, this will not affect the sense of the discussions. If it were assumed that the model was operating with a policy similar to that observed in Section 38 of Chapter II, the aggregate demand would respond to control subsidies or depression of Ep in the same way as it does when the probable mode is assumed.

APPENDIX A

GLOSSARY

accelerated growth rate — See Section 12 of Chapter II.

aggregate demand — The aggregate demand is equal in magnitude to the gross national product. Unless otherwise indicated, the measure of aggregate demand is always in *current* dollars, as opposed to constant, or adjusted, dollars; unless otherwise indicated, the rate existing at any time is implied, as opposed to the volume over some period. The aggregate demand may be looked upon as the rate of expenditures for all finished goods and services by the ultimate users plus the rate of increase in merchandise inventories.

alignment of demand — See Section 10 of Chapter II.

control subsidies — The amount of control subsidies in any period is the amount of revenues lost to the government by virtue of the tax on the first income bracket being below the normal value. The rate of control subsidies in use at any time is usually expressed as a percentage of the (rate of) aggregate demand.

controlled economy — See Section 2 of Chapter II.

d — See Section 23 of Chapter II.

Eg — This is the rate of increase in the total amount of government bonds held by the banks. For most discussions it is assumed that the total amount of government bonds held by individuals other than banks remains constant. Under this simplification, Eg is also the rate at which the government issues bonds. This quantity is usually expressed as a percentage of the (rate of) aggregate demand.

Ep — This is the total rate of bank credit expansion minus that portion due to the increase in government bonds held by the banks. This quantity is usually expressed as a percentage of the (rate of) aggregate demand.

flexible tax — This is the variable tax rate on the first income bracket as described in Section 16 of Chapter II.

functional causes of depressions — See Section 29 of Chapter II.

inflation — By inflation is meant any rise of the price index applying to the gross national product. The rate of inflation is the rate of rise of the price index in percent per year.

international trade — This term is used loosely to embrace all transactions entering into the balance of international payments.

lowest realizable interest rate — See Section 28 of Chapter II.

money — The total money of the economy includes all currency in circulation outside of the banks and all demand deposits, or checking accounts.

muney — The total muney of the economy includes all currency in circulation outside of the banks and all bank deposits, whether they be checking accounts or savings accounts.

muney-savings — For any individual the rate of muney-savings is the rate at which the muney he owns rises. For the economy as a whole the rate of muney-saving is the sum of the rates of all individuals, and this must be the rate at which the total muney of the economy increases.

neutral balance of payments — By a neutral balance of international payments is meant one in which there is neither a surplus nor deficit.

new-muney-rate — This is the rate at which the total muney of the economy increases. This quantity is usually expressed as a percentage of the (rate of) aggregate demand.

non-controlled economy — See Section 2 of Chapter II.

normal rate of budgetary surplus — This is the rate of budgetary surplus that occurs when the flexible tax rate is at the normal value.

normal rate of Ep — This is the value to which Ep is restricted when downward corrections of the aggregate demand are not required, assuming that the control policy outlined in Section 18 of Chapter II is being employed.

normal value of flexible tax — This is the value assigned by the legislature to provide for an equitable tax burden on the first income bracket. It is also the maximum value of the flexible tax, the executive being empowered to make the flexible tax lower than this rate but not higher.

output — The output of the economy as a whole is equal in magnitude to the gross national product. Unless otherwise indicated the output of the economy is always in *real* measure, such as constant, or adjusted, dollars; unless otherwise indicated, the rate existing at any time is implied, as opposed to the volume over some period. The output per worker also implies a rate in real measure.

planning cushion — See Section 3 of Chapter II.

probable mode of operation — See Section 28 of Chapter II.

propensity-to-save-muney — See PSM.

PSM — The PSM (propensity-to-save-muney) is the new-muney-rate that is required, or would be required, to keep the aggregate demand constant. This quantity is ordinarily expressed as a percentage of the (rate of) aggregate demand.

(PSM + d) — The (PSM + d) is the new-muney-rate that is required, or would be required, to keep the aggregate demand on the desired curve. This quantity is ordinarily expressed as a percentage of the (rate of) aggregate demand.

psychosomatic behavior — See Section 29 of Chapter II.

R — This is the ratio of the total muney of the economy to the aggregate demand when the latter quantity is in current dollars per year.

tariff-subsidy rate — See Section 13 of Chapter II.

utilization rate — See Chapter V, Section 1.

Z — This is the rate of rise of the desired aggregate demand curve in percent per year.

[illegible] — This is the value to which [illegible] is restricted [illegible] the aggregate demand [illegible] control policy outlined in Section 12 [illegible] being used.

[illegible] value of flexible tax. — This is the value required by the [illegible] or a [illegible] tax [illegible] that [illegible] the maximum value of the flexible [illegible] to make the [illegible] not [illegible] higher.

[illegible]. — The output of the economy as a whole is equal to total [illegible]. Unless otherwise [illegible] always [illegible] measures, such as [illegible] dollars unless otherwise indicated. [illegible] is implied, as opposed to the volume [illegible]. The output per worker also implies a rate [illegible].

[illegible]. — See Section 1 of Chapter II.

[illegible]. — See Section 25 of Chapter III.

[illegible]. — [illegible] PSM.

PSM. — The PSM ([illegible]) is the [illegible] that would be [illegible] the aggregate [illegible] is [illegible] expressed as a [illegible] of the [illegible] aggregate demand.

(PSM + [illegible]). — The (PSM + [illegible]) is the [illegible] rate that [illegible] to keep the aggregate demand [illegible]. This quantity is [illegible] expressed as a percentage of [illegible] aggregate demand.

[illegible] behavior. — See Section 27 of Chapter II.

[illegible] — [illegible] is the ratio of the total money of the economy to the [illegible] the latter quantity [illegible] current dollars.

[illegible]. — See Section 13 of Chapter II.

[illegible] rate. — See Chapter V, Section 1.

Z. — This is the rate of rise of the desired aggregate demand curve, [illegible] per cent per year.

DATE DUE

APR 17 '64

GAYLORD

PRINTED IN U.S.A.